THE YEAR I
GOT EVERYTHING I
WANTED

NAVPRESS DELIBERATE

From the very beginning, God created humans to love Him and each other. He intended for His people to be a blessing to everyone on earth so that everyone would know Him (see Genesis 12:2). Jesus also taught this over and over and promised to give His people all they needed to make it happen — His resources, His power, and His presence (see Matthew 28:20; John 14:12-14). NavPress Deliberate takes Him at His word and stirs its readers to do the same — to be the children of God for whom creation is groaning to be revealed. We have only to glance through the Bible to discover what it looks like to be the blessing God has intended: caring for the poor, orphan, widow, prisoner, and foreigner (see Micah 6:8; Matthew 25:31-46; Isaiah 58); and redeeming the world — everyone and everything in it (see Colossians 1:19-20; Romans 8:19-23).

NavPress Deliberate encourages readers to embrace this holistic and vibrant Christian faith: It is both contemplative and active; it unites mystery-embracing faith with theological rootedness; it breaks down the sacred/secular divide, recognizing God's sovereignty and redemptive work in every facet of life; it dialogues with other faiths and worldviews and embraces God's truth found there; it creates culture and uses artistic ability to unflinchingly tell the truth about this life and God's redemption of it; it fosters a faith bold enough to incarnate the gospel in a shrinking and diverse world. NavPress Deliberate is for everyone on a pilgrimage to become like Jesus and to continue His work of living and discipling among all people.

Become what you believe.
The NavPress Deliberate Team

THE YEAR I GOT EVERYTHING I WANTED

A SPIRITUAL CRISIS

CAMERON CONANT

NAVPRESS

The Navigators is an international Christian organization. Our mission is to advance the gospel of Jesus and His kingdom into the nations through spiritual generations of laborers living and discipling among the lost. We see a vital movement of the gospel, fueled by prevailing prayer, flowing freely through relational networks and out into the nations where workers for the kingdom are next door to everywhere.

NavPress is the publishing ministry of The Navigators. The mission of NavPress is to reach, disciple, and equip people to know Christ and make Him known by publishing life-related materials that are biblically rooted and culturally relevant. Our vision is to stimulate spiritual transformation through every product we publish.

© 2007 by Cameron Conant

All rights reserved. No part of this publication may be reproduced in any form without written permission from NavPress, P.O. Box 35001, Colorado Springs, CO 80935. www.navpress.com

NAVPRESS, BRINGING TRUTH TO LIFE, and the NAVPRESS logo are registered trademarks of NavPress. Absence of ® in connection with marks of NavPress or other parties does not indicate an absence of registration of those marks.

ISBN-13: 978-1-60006-145-5
ISBN-10: 1-60006-145-1

Cover design by studiogearbox.com
Cover image by Getty/Charles Gullung
Author photo by Rory White, www.rorywhite.com
Creative Team: Andrea Christian, Caleb Seeling, Darla Hightower, Arvid Wallen, Kathy Guist

Some of the anecdotal illustrations in this book are true to life and are included with the permission of the persons involved. All other illustrations are composites of real situations, and any resemblance to people living or dead is coincidental.

Unless otherwise identified, all Scripture quotations in this publication are taken from Today's New International® Version (TNIV)®. Copyright 2001, 2005 by International Bible Society®. All rights reserved worldwide. Other versions used include: *THE MESSAGE* (MSG). Copyright © 1993, 1994, 1995, 1996, 2000, 2001, 2002, 2005. Used by permission of NavPress Publishing Group.

Conant, Cameron.
  The year I got everything I wanted : a spiritual crisis / Cameron Conant.
      p. cm.
  Includes bibliographical references.
  ISBN-13: 978-1-60006-145-5
  ISBN-10: 1-60006-145-1
  1. Conant, Cameron. 2. Spiritual biography. 3. Bible. O.T. Ecclesiastes--Criticism, interpretation, etc. I. Title.
  BR1725.C56A3 2007
  277.3'083092--dc22
  [B]
                                            2007015660

Printed in the United States of America

1 2 3 4 5 6 7 8 / 11 10 09 08 07

FOR A FREE CATALOG OF NAVPRESS BOOKS & BIBLE STUDIES, CALL
1-800-366-7788 (USA) OR 1-800-839-4769 (CANADA).

For Sally Chambers

CONTENTS

ACKNOWLEDGMENTS

Special thanks go to Andrea Christian, my gifted editor and trusted friend, as well as to my parents, Dennis and Jana, people of grace and warmth, and to my brother, Christian, and sister, Alissa, both siblings and friends. To Drew Tilghman, a friend of great worth and wisdom, to Caroline Craddock, a dear friend and gifted writer, to Sally Chambers, a spiritual hero who is always there to listen, and to Rory White, my wonderful friend and neighbor.

Special thanks also go to Rob Stewart for his wise counsel and unfailing friendship, and to Melinda Van Kirk, who has seen me through good times and bad. I am also grateful to other friends who helped me in my twenty-eighth year, people such as Matthew Paul Turner, Stephen and Melanie Bryant, Shane Baker, Ashley Earnhardt, Bethany Neff, Aaron Carriere, Adria Haley, Doc and Julie Martin, Tammi Gray, Derek VanderWeide, Vicki Cessna, Karen Campbell, Leslie Speyers, Kim Zeilstra, Sarah Streck, Almis Udrys, and those who visit my blog on a regular basis. Thanks also to the late Rob Lacey, who inspires me to keep going.

I am also indebted to Mary Groom, the entire NavPress team, and the Deremo and Conant families. Thanks also to readers who have e-mailed me — little did you know that many days you gave me the courage to keep writing. I am incredibly grateful to the faith community of St. Bartholomew's, Nashville, and especially grateful for the one who gave me breath, and words, and a song to sing. I hope, one day, to sing it well.

INTRODUCTION

When thinking of a title for this book, I came up with a terribly awkward one: *The Year of Unfulfilled Longing.* When I said it, people raised their eyebrows and swallowed hard and tried to say nice things, but it was a bad idea—they knew it, I knew it. Saying it now, it sounds terrible, really terrible, but that's how I felt then—that I had this longing, this hole, this void, and I desperately wanted to fill it. But then I realized that my twenty-eighth year was really the year I got everything I wanted, which also made for a better book title. And it's true; I really did get everything I wanted, the only problem being that getting those things proved depressing. I thought a new job, a new girlfriend, moving to a new city, and having my first book published would fill a void, but none of it did. And when it didn't, I hardly knew what to do with myself.

During my twenty-eighth year, I thought a lot about another book, not this one, but one called Ecclesiastes. If you've never read it, Ecclesiastes is strange and says all sorts of things about how life is meaningless and empty and that there's only one thing that counts. It's an old book, happens to be in the Bible, and is written — at least some think — by Solomon, the ancient king of Israel and supposedly the wisest man to ever live.

A lot of people think the Bible is pretty irrelevant, and I can understand why. It's this weird anthology of writings from thousands of years ago, and at the end of a long day, who wants to read an anthology? I'd rather read *Time* or maybe the latest Frank McCourt book, not some obscure leather-bound manifesto about this God who the Jews worshipped and Christians adopted. This God who seems so distant sometimes. But there was something about Ecclesiastes that kept me coming back. Not only did it seem naked and vulnerable and honest, it told me something about myself.

The brilliant poet and writer Eugene Peterson says, "Ecclesiastes actually doesn't say that much about God; the author leaves that to the other sixty-five books of the Bible. His task is to expose our total incapacity to find the meaning and completion of our lives on our own."[1] When I read this, it made sense why I liked Ecclesiastes so much. It exposed me — not in a condescending, finger-wagging way, but in the way my favorite song exposes me or my favorite poem does. It exposed everything about my twenty-eighth year — the striving, the doing, the misplaced hopes and dreams, the selfishness — and at the end of that year, I, like Solomon, could only admit my inability to find happiness or meaning on my own. I needed God — that obscure figure who sometimes seemed so far away, so mysterious, so frustrating, and now, suddenly, so entirely necessary.

This book is a memoir, but in a bigger sense, it's a personal reflection on Ecclesiastes, or perhaps better stated, a personal journey through Ecclesiastes. I've pulled thoughts and ideas from that old book and wrapped them around this new one in a mostly subtle way. And I hope it works, hope it means something, and hope, most of all, this story is true and honest and full, just as I've found Solomon's to be.

I say true and honest and full, but let me say a word about memoirs, which, due to one book in particular, have generated a fair amount of discussion these past few years. The book you're holding now is, like all memoirs, memory based. That means that when I wrote it, I didn't make phone calls and talk to eye witnesses and fact-check every detail, all of which I would've done in my former career as a newspaper reporter.

Not only did I not fact-check every detail, some names and details were actually altered to protect those who wouldn't want to be mentioned. However, I can say with confidence that the integrity of this story is fully intact and, in fact, the bulk of this book is so real that in writing it, I was often uncomfortable with my own transparency, and still am.

Most of the main characters in this book had a chance to read the manuscript before it went to print—even those who are no longer a part of my life, even those whose names were altered—because my intent was never to smear or hurt or defame or diminish. It seems strange telling you all of this, how I wrote the book, what my intentions were, but I've found that two virtues God values most are humility and honesty.

I pray this book contains both.

CHAPTER 1

A TIME TO SEARCH

The last and final word is this: Fear God. Do what he tells you. And that's it. Eventually God will bring everything that we do out into the open and judge it according to its hidden intent, whether it's good or evil.[1]

I just turned twenty-nine.

Ten seconds ago, I turned twenty-nine.

There are no balloons, streamers, or well-wishers.

There is only the click-clack of train wheels and the sound of wind.

I am headed to Prague but currently breezing through Germany. It's midnight, July 11, 2006, and I'm not quite to Würzburg. Across from me, a pouty-faced eighteen-year-old from Park City, Utah, sleeps with his mouth open. To my right, his friend, eyes closed, holds an iPod in his hand, its dim, bluish light splashed across his mouth and chin.

These soon-to-be college freshmen look like babies to me, and I think of all the things that happen between eighteen and twenty-eight, a decade of transition from child to adult.

The cabin is dark, the window open, the curtains blowing like bedsheets on a clothesline. The train chases the moon, which casts surprisingly little light on the farms and villages we pass. Occasionally, we zip through a tunnel, and in some strange way, the dark graffiti reminds me of prehistoric cave drawings — attempts to express something, tell a story, or leave a mark.

The need to express something is intrinsic to being human, and the reason I wrote my first memoir at fifteen years old — a four-page lament on how I got cut from my high school basketball team. I didn't write it because I wanted to; I wrote it because I couldn't *not* write it, which is the same reason I sit here tonight, writing a sentence or two every few minutes in my black Moleskine notebook.

I put the journal down and zip up my green sweatshirt. Leaning my head back, I look out the window and watch shadows dance across the landscape. I try and make sense of the movement. What am I doing on a midnight train to Prague on my birthday? What was the point of my last year — the year I got everything I wanted?

It all seems surreal. I feel as if I've lived someone else's life, but no, it's mine, I'm sure of that. Well, most of the time I am. I'm twenty-nine now, but I still remember that summer day when I walked into my apartment and found half the furniture gone, a typed note on the kitchen table with two keys placed next to it. "I'm filing for divorce," it said.

Welcome to twenty-seven.

Those first months of twenty-seven stretched forever, the gray hair appearing, the married friends disappearing, the secondhand television with the baseball game always on. I eventually moved on, got a new television, made new friends, and moved to a new city. But tonight — the wind in my hair, the two Utah kids asleep — I keep going backward.

I was just a child the fall day I saw her from across the college quad, just a child when I circled her picture in the book of freshmen. I was as innocent as the slack-jawed, pouty-faced kid across from me sleeping his way through the German countryside. I was innocent enough to believe the dream, the stereotypical American one that says you go to college and marry the sorority girl and get a good job and raise three cute kids in the suburban house with a bigger backyard than your neighbors have. In this dream, you keep problems to yourself and let everyone know how great your life is. But that dream not only got abandoned, it got detonated with explosives powerful enough to bring down those ugly, almost indestructible American sports stadiums, the ones that played across my television screen the summer my wife left.

When I think of twenty-seven, I remember how big my bed was for those first few months, but after a while, just how small it seemed. By the end of twenty-seven, I stopped reaching for my wife when I rolled over at night. By then, I couldn't even smell her anymore, not even in the dresser drawer where she once kept perfume-scented clothes fresheners.

I smelled something else: success, my first book deal, a $2,500 advance — not enough to retire on, but, hey, I was about to be an author. I even had publicity photos taken in downtown Grand Rapids. How many people have publicity photos taken in downtown Grand Rapids? *Not many*, I thought. *Not many*. I was going to be someone in Grand Rapids.

I also had a couple of radio interviews lined up, which amazed me. *These people want to hear what I have to say? I'm no one*, I thought. I wondered if I should tell them, "Look, before we do this, you just need to know that I wrote this thing on the weekends at Schuler Books & Music on Twenty-eighth Street, and, well, I'll be happy if someone other than my mom buys it."

I would have to wait until twenty-eight to find out if someone would.

I turned twenty-eight only 365 days ago, but I wasn't on a midnight train to Prague. Instead, I sat in a skyscraper overlooking the Rocky Mountains, eating dinner with a woman named Hope, a woman who occasionally kissed me. I was the new author from Grand Rapids with dark, spiky hair; she was the Nashville girl with the big sunglasses, designer jeans, and form-fitting business jackets.

I tried to remember which fork to use as we sat there with our salads waiting for roast duck or some other delicacy I didn't really want. I remember putting the thick napkin on my lap and saying in a voice just louder than a whisper, "The other day I almost called you my girlfr— well, you know." "I know," she said, smiling. We hadn't defined what we were calling our kisses, this dinner, the late-night phone calls, but I prayed that I might one day call her my— well, you know.

There is so much I could say about her: how her hair looked like fields of wheat in the late summer sun, how she blushed every time I did my impression of Richard Marx singing "Should've Known Better," how upon reading my first book, she shook her head and told me my ex-wife was crazy. "You had me at, 'She was crazy,'" I wanted to say.

I think my ex-wife could've said I was crazy. I did a lot of stupid things to escape my pain at twenty-eight. Not just kissing Hope and moving to Nashville less than a year after my divorce, but other things too. Things like taking a job with a great salary and impressive title, a job I knew I wasn't interested in doing, a job that turned out to be as comfortable as too-small burlap underwear. I had been so hurt for so long that I just wanted to be happy. And isn't that what life's about? Parents say it all the time — "I just want her to be happy" — and I think this makes sense. Happiness is a good thing, and as an American I'm entitled to life, liberty, and the pursuit of happiness, right?

I thought I would be happy with more money, an impressive job title, and a beautiful girlfriend with wheat-colored hair who wore designer jeans. I thought I would be happy living in Nashville, a place where people went to coffee shops and looked hauntingly artistic in tight T-shirts.

I wasn't.

Hope and I broke up three days after Christmas — one week after I gave her two dining room table chairs that cost $1,200. The day I purchased them, one of her best friends pleaded with me to buy her towels, or a shirt, or, at the most, just one chair. "Cameron, don't do it; just give her one of the chairs, not two. That's so much money." I suddenly imagined the two of us in a movie, her saying, "Cameron, cut the green wire first . . . for heaven's sake, cut the green wire!" I couldn't help myself. I cut the red wire. Hope liked nice things. I liked Hope.

One February night, I found myself going a hundred miles per hour down the freeway, orange construction barrels to my right and left. Learning of this the next day, my mom was beside herself. "Cam, you need to change your self-talk! This isn't the end of the world."

It felt like it.

Then I met Erica, a tall, beautiful blonde who often wore flat shoes so she wouldn't tower over me. She wasn't the sort of girl who wanted $1,200 chairs. She was the sort of girl who brought you a sandwich when you had to go straight from work to defensive driving school because you got a speeding ticket — fortunately not one for going a hundred miles per hour in a construction zone. And then one day, I shocked her, told her that I couldn't date her anymore, that I had to leave, that I was going to Europe, quitting my job, maybe never coming back to Nashville. She wanted to come. I told her to stay.

In the weeks that followed, I fell into a deep depression, wondered how I would climb out of it, wondered what the point was anymore. I ended up going home weeks before my flight to Europe, sitting with my dad, watching baseball on television.

And now here I am, seven days into a ten-week journey through Europe, and I'm reminded of something. I'm reminded of the fact that I'm a Christian. I tell you that because the road toward the heart of God is the greatest journey I've ever taken and the subtext for every story I could ever tell you. It's the subtext for this trip to Europe, the subtext for the year I got everything I wanted.

I must admit that it's a bit intimidating to tell you that I'm a Christian — well maybe not to tell *you*, but perhaps to tell your friend, or my aunt, or anyone else who sees all of the contradictions more clearly than I do.

There's no escaping the fact that the word *Christian* has been perverted — perverted by people who are unfortunately a lot like me — people who sometimes use the Bible to defend their own positions, their own insecurities, their own interests. Perverted by people who use the Bible as a scientific treatise, a political playbook, or something that should be used to crush the spirits, and sometimes bodies, of people who don't believe.

On some level, I understand why this happens. The Bible is a complicated book written over thousands of years by dozens of different people. It's a series of stories, each told within a certain cultural context for a certain audience. There's a lot to sort through, a lot to wrestle with, and unfortunately some people don't like to wrestle. But tonight, I'm ready. For the first time in months, my spirit is prepared to chew on questions that too often get pushed away like cake after three plates of spaghetti.

Questions like: Does the Bible have anything to say to a twenty-nine-year-old on a midnight train to Prague? Does it have anything to say to someone with little idea of where he is, where he's going, or where he's been?

I say I'm a Christian, but sometimes I wonder about that. Take this pouty-faced kid across from me for example. We spoke before the train left from Frankfurt, Germany, and I instantly disliked him, almost hated him. Why? He wasn't friendly. He frowned. He seemed distant. The poor guy was probably just exhausted, but I was irritated with how he greeted me. I thought, *Oh, Park City, Utah, sure. I know kids like you. You're some pampered country club brat with expensive ski equipment and a summer home in Tahoe where you take sixteen-year-old girls.*

I honestly thought these things, which probably isn't what you'd expect from a Christian. Or, sadly, maybe it is. Of course I could tell you things much worse than that, not things you've heard in church, like, "I've just been so impatient with my kids lately and I have a cold." No, I'm thinking of dark things, things you don't say in polite company. I'm thinking of pornography, jealousy, lust, gossip, and deception — things that are really ugly. Things that are a part of me.

I have a lot of darkness inside of me, but as the author Parker

Palmer says, "To embrace weakness, liability, and darkness as part of who I am gives that part less sway over me, because all it ever wanted was to be acknowledged as part of my whole self."[2] I think that's true. I acknowledge my tendency to live my worst life now, acknowledge that I'm not a very good person sometimes, that I have the ability to do very bad things. But I also acknowledge that I have the ability to do very good things. It's all a part of me—freshwater and saltwater, light and dark. This shouldn't be, but it is.

In fact, the apostle Paul says, "I decide one way, but then I act another."[3] I know, Paul. I do too. I think Solomon, the ancient king of Israel and supposedly the wisest man to ever live, could identify with Paul and me. Solomon tells this story in the biblical book of Ecclesiastes about how he got everything he wanted but found it all wanting, all meaningless, all just a "chasing after the wind."[4]

I don't know who let Ecclesiastes in the Bible, but let's not talk about it too much in public so certain religious leaders don't mount a campaign against it, or the government doesn't slap a label on it, because I swear it's pretty subversive. It says things like, there's "a time to hate"[5] and "a time to destroy."[6] Really?

A quick survey of Solomon's life shows he probably had lots of sex, drank his share of wine, built God's temple, and had all the riches he could ever want. But for some reason, none of it made him all that happy. Why? Was Solomon self-centered? The wisest man who ever lived, self-centered? Is it possible? I think it is. I mean, the guy lived a full-tilt, pleasure-seeking lifestyle. He wasn't Mother Teresa getting up at 5 a.m. to say prayers and then spending twelve hours with people who had skin falling off of their bones.

Something tells me Solomon's failures could teach me a thing or two. My twenty-eighth year was 365 days of serving myself. It was a treasure hunt for the elusive "it." I was constantly plotting, reevaluating. Ten paces here, four paces there, digging under this tree, looking under this stone or in that cave. And in the end, I found myself without a shovel or treasure map, just a two-month ticket to ride virtually any train in Europe, everything I needed in a backpack.

As I look out the window tonight, we fly past a train station, its bright lights illuminating our small cabin for a moment. As the light flickers like a movie reel, my watch casts a beam of light onto the forehead of the pouty-faced kid.

I have lived Solomon's life, I think to myself, staring at the dab of light.

No, I didn't have his money or his women—certainly didn't have as much sex as he had—all those concubines—but I have lived his life. I know what it feels like to come to the end of myself and ask, "Is this it? Really? Is this all there is?" Life is so vacuous when I live for myself—a black hole that sucks up everything in its path. When I live only for myself, I become a consumer first and foremost—a consumer of products, emotions, and ideas. And when I do produce something, it resembles a Styrofoam Big Mac container or a bad pop song—throwaway things that never disintegrate.

In Ecclesiastes, Solomon writes, "The last and final word is this: Fear God. Do what he tells you. And that's it. Eventually God will bring everything that we do out into the open and judge it according to its hidden intent, whether it's good or evil."[7]

Solomon's conclusion after a life of getting and doing everything he wants is this: disempowerment. Think of what Solomon is saying: Fear. *Do. Listen. Go.* Revenge and self-rationalization are taken away. The need to explain ourselves disappears because God (not us) will make everything known.

Still, even in telling you this story, I want to look good in your eyes. *Okay, I'll tell you the bad things first, but by the end, you'll be sticking up for me. You'll think I'm good. You'll like me. You'll accept me.* This is how I think sometimes. *Well, I know it looked like this, but this is what I was thinking. This is what really happened.*

But Solomon points us to the true source of happiness, which isn't found in trying to control this roller coaster, but in loving and obeying the one who has the qualifications to drive it, the one who built it in the first place. Solomon's conclusion after a life of pleasure seeking is "Do what he tells you." *Wow. What he tells me? What's that?* I don't hear anything tonight but wheels and wind and my own internal monologue.

But that's okay. I'm finally ready to listen. Yeah, *after* the year I got everything I wanted, I'm finally ready.

I look around, the cabin dark, and smile at the pouty-faced kid. He can't see me, but I smile.

Sorry, I think to myself. *Sorry.*

CHAPTER 2

A TIME TO EMBRACE

Remember your Creator in the days of your youth, before the days of trouble come and the years approach when you will say, "I find no pleasure in them."[1]

It's July 11, 2005, and I'm in downtown Denver walking toward the Colorado Convention Center. It's only 9 a.m. but already eighty-five degrees. Everything is covered in a reddish-orange haze — the sort of light that dances around your eyes after you've looked at the sun too long. I'm wearing a long-sleeved blue dress shirt and carrying a notebook under my arm.

It's supposed to be ninety-five degrees today, and I'm already sweating through the armpits of this shirt. I've only walked one block and I'm wondering if I should've taken the shuttle, but come on, it's five blocks, I can walk.

I'm celebrating my twenty-eighth birthday today at this convention — the biggest Christian book convention of the year. There are mainly books at this show, but there are other things as well, including Christian clothes, Christian candy, and a wall of Christian dolls.

Yesterday I saw a Christian T-shirt with an imitation Mountain Dew logo on it and the words "He Died for You!" emblazoned across the front. In another area I found Christian breath mints called "Testamints" with Bible verses on them, the idea being that you can share Jesus with someone and improve their breath at the same time. I thought their slogan should be, "Jesus loves you! But he'd love you more with fresh breath." I even saw a Christian board game with marketing copy that read, "The player closest to Jesus wins."

Retailers from around the country are at this convention to order new products, hear authors speak, and attend talks on how to increase sales. I'm here because I'm the public relations manager for a large Christian publishing company where I promote Christian books and Bibles.

I promote the Bible.

What this means is when we publish a new Bible, I write a press release, send it to reporters and editors, and then try to get them to mention our "product" on their show or in their magazine. I went from being a newspaper reporter, interviewing people like Charlie Daniels ("Why *did* the devil go down to Georgia?" I asked him, thinking I was clever, though I was probably the millionth reporter to ask that question) to promoting the Bible. But the newspaper paid only $24,000 per year. The Bible pays better.

You may not be aware of this, but there are all sorts of Bibles. Not just the super boring black hardcover ones you remember seeing as a kid, but Bibles with study notes, Bibles with devotional insights written by pastors, Bibles with funky covers that match your girlfriend's purse, sports Bibles that look like basketballs, square-shaped Bibles, Bibles that hold photos in the front, Bibles with zippers and snaps and magnetic clasps, and even audio Bibles read by famous people. If this weren't strange enough, there are well over a dozen English-language Bible translations, all of which are known by acronyms: NIV (New International Version), TNIV (Today's New International Version), KJV (King James Version), NRSV (New Revised Standard Version), NASB (New American Standard Bible) . . . the list goes on and on.

So someone could conceivably say, "You know, I have an NASB study Bible with a turquoise cover, but what I'd *really* like is a square NRSV Bible with devotional insights and a pink synthetic leather cover with a magnetic clasp."

I know this is weird. Some people find it weird that we even sell the Bible, let alone make it with clasps and pockets. I remember as a newspaper reporter having a conversation with my editor about this, one in which he said Christianity was all about slick marketing, nothing else.

I wanted to tell him the Spirit moves in mysterious ways, wanted to tell him that Muslims were having dreams about Jesus in places where they couldn't buy Testamints or Bibles with magnetic clasps or even boring black hardcover Bibles. I wanted to tell him that these dreams were real. These messages weren't sponsored by Christian soft-drink T-shirts; these messages were mystical, strange, bizarre, inexplicable.

But too often, I look around and wonder if maybe my editor isn't right. I wonder if Christianity hasn't become all about slick marketing, at least in America, home of the "Would you like an extra burger with your order for only $1.99?" We even have a tendency to worship capitalism in church. "Listen to my sermon, and, oh by the way, have you seen my book? It's at the bottom of your television screen. We also sell an accompanying journal." I sometimes have Orwellian visions of megapastors installing credit card scanners on their pews so anytime congregants hear of a book or product that piques their interest, they simply swipe their cards and pick up their purchase in the lobby afterward.

I have a feeling my editor has those same visions.

In my editor's mind, Jesus is probably the best marketer to ever live, and knowing the tens of thousands of books published each year, there must be a book on how Jesus can teach us marketing principles, as well as books on how Jesus can teach us to be better cooks, landscapers, and skiers.

This sort of thing makes my stomach turn — and would even more so if I didn't know so many wonderful people who sell and write Christian books, books that sometimes strike me — sensitive, antimarketing me — as a bit crass. I even know wonderful people who sell Christian dolls and Testamints and "He Died for You!" soft-drink T-shirts. So I can't throw stones — I'm in no position to. In fact, on some level I'm a hypocrite for even pointing this all out.

You see, just like this blue shirt sticking to my back, I'm stuck in this weird evangelical Christian subculture — willingly stuck. Not only do I work for a Christian publisher but I'm also now an author — in fact, an advance copy of my book, *With or Without You*, is on display in one of the booths at this very convention. I must admit that I'm proud of this. A small, progressive company is publishing the book. And, well, it's a book, and that alone makes me feel important. Even in an industry where everyone writes books, I feel significant — something that would've been unimaginable during my four-year marriage, a time when my confidence was so low I had difficulty even looking people in the eye.

But now I'm someone.

I can picture in my head where my publisher's booth is on the show floor. I imagine how I'll discreetly walk by and glance at the cover for the thirtieth time in two days. It's my birthday and the least I can do for myself—revel in the accomplishment of finishing an entire book. However, I must admit that I always pictured writing something like *To Kill a Mockingbird*, not a divorce memoir that talks about masturbation and pornography and how my wife left in the stereotypical way: a typed letter on the kitchen table.

Yet when I get into the convention center, I still hope people point and whisper, "There's Cameron. Oh, have you heard about his book? It's really edgy and brave."

But it's not just the book that I'm excited about at this convention . . . there's also a girl.

Hope looks like a model: petite, but surprisingly tall in heels; bleached hair that looks like a field of wheat in the late afternoon sun. She wears business suits that fit much better than the ones women wear in Grand Rapids, especially this one that's white. When she wears it, it's impossible not to notice her because she looks like Princess Diana. At least I think so.

But it's not just Hope's wardrobe that has me daydreaming this morning. Hope sometimes smiles at me, looks away, then blushes, and I immediately fall into a trance and begin agreeing with everything she says. "I think that's stupid, Cameron." "Yes, I agree, Hope." "I'm tired, Cameron." "Yes, me too, Hope." "I want to get a burrito, Cameron." "A burrito sounds great, Hope, even at seven in the morning." But it's not just me. When Hope walks into a restaurant, every male turns his head and stares at her. I swear, half the restaurant could be on fire—people screaming, trampling each other—and firemen would put down their equipment, flames going up their pant legs, and just look at Hope.

There are all sorts of interesting things about Hope, the first being she's interested in me. I can't believe it. I honestly thought that no one would ever date me again after my divorce, or maybe someone would, but she would be really weird, like a girl who picked her nose, had twelve kids, and lived in an RV.

Hope is creative and smart, always looks like she walked out of a magazine, runs her own graphic design company, is my age, has never been married, and just happens to be at this convention. She likes to shop, can drop $500 like it's $5, and has a huge white dog that jumps on the couch and whines. She talks with a beautiful Southern accent where "ten" sounds like "tin." Most interesting of all, Hope's parents are marriage therapists, which is a great storyline for a romantic comedy. I sometimes imagine them grumbling about their wild daughter, the one interested in that divorced guy who just happens to be from the North.

In the movie though, I would be funny and sweet and endearing and would undoubtedly do something cute that would make those Southern therapists like me. In the movie, I would be so romantic that I would ask Hope to marry me while ice-skating in New York City, and everyone would hear my proposal and start clapping. And as they clapped, snow gently falling, Hope and I would kiss, and then one of those guys who drives the horse-drawn carriages around Central Park would give us a free ride.

It would be nice if life turned out like that movie, because I think I could marry Hope. We've been talking only for about four months, but there's something about her that makes me stare at my bedroom ceiling at two in the morning, and I don't think it's just her legs, or her full lips, or that wheat-colored hair, though I have certainly noticed those things. Above anything else, I'm a sucker for chemistry, which Hope and I have—I knew it the first time I met her at dinner earlier this spring when a business colleague and I were in Nashville. My colleague suggested it, and I didn't argue. I had seen Hope before but never really talked to her. Now it would be just the three of us at dinner. That night I kept looking at her, and she kept looking down at her plate, and I kept looking at her, and she would finally look up at me, her eyes dancing. I felt as if someone had rubbed Icy Hot over my entire body, especially after I discovered that we both had the same favorite movie: *Casablanca*, a strange choice for two people in their late twenties.

I also learned something else shortly after meeting Hope. I learned that her therapist father had written a book on divorce and marital separation—the same book my mom had given me when my wife and I were separated before our divorce, almost two years before I ever knew Hope. *God, is this a sign? I know I'm a little slow on the uptake sometimes, but this is just, well, weird*, I thought at the time, and still think.

Hope's father also wrote a book about . . . Hope! Yes, you can order it, Hope and her dad on the back cover, father and daughter in a half embrace, standing in front of a fall oak tree. The book is titled *To My Little Girl: A Father's Relationship Advice to His Daughter*. I found a copy one day and started searching for the part where he says, "Look out for divorced guys . . . they're shady . . . especially divorced guys with dark, spiky hair from the liberal North."

I live in Grand Rapids, Michigan, right now, but I've been thinking about moving to Nashville, which is where Hope lives. Grand Rapids isn't a bad place, and, in fact, it might be the best city in Michigan. There are good restaurants, friendly people, concerts, semiprofessional sports teams, and great beaches only forty minutes away. There is a river called the Grand that cuts right through the center of downtown, but it might be grand only if you've never seen a river. And no offense to the city forefathers, but the rapids aren't exactly rapid, certainly not something you'd see in a white-water rafting brochure. If I had to rename the city, I might call it Not-Too-Exciting Midwestern River.

Grand Rapids is a family town, a place where people have potluck suppers, attend church Bible studies on Wednesdays, and pronounce things through their nose, but not in a pretty way like the French do. "Greeend Reeepids" (translation: "Grand Rapids"). "Cowledge" (translation: "College").

Grand Rapids is a place where it's a bit strange to be twenty-eight and single—or, worse yet, divorced—a place where it's a bit strange to be me. I'm an outsider in a city that traces its roots to Dutch settlers who stayed for the farmland and close proximity to water. Today, a look through the Grand Rapids phone book still turns up tens of thousands of Dutch names like Hoekstra, Van Andel, and DeVos. But Conant? Nowhere to be found. Conant is a distinguished name, or so I tell myself, but it's not Dutch. And according to a phrase I heard in Grand Rapids once, "If you ain't Dutch, you ain't much." Grand Rapids might be the only place in America where someone would laugh if you said that.

I read a book about Paul Revere once that mentioned a General Conant who fought in the Revolutionary War, so I started telling people that my family had been in America since then—much longer than the Grand Rapids Dutch, but, crap, there was that Dutchman Peter Stuyvesant—early settler of Manhattan and governor of the Dutch colony once known as New Amsterdam, later New York, so the Dutch had been here a while too. I had to do a book report on Peter Stuyvesant when I was in third grade, but I never read the book and began sweating when called to stand in front of the class and expound on the virtues of the Dutchman Stuyvesant. Not only did I butcher his name, I had nothing to say. I remember mumbling a few non-sensical things and then sitting down, wishing the earth would open and swallow me along with my desk, Trapper Keeper, and pencil box. Kids laughed, the teacher scowled at me from behind her grade book, and I stared at the floor, waiting for God to take me then and there.

My dad once said we were Scotch-Irish, so I've incorporated it into my non-Dutch history, along with a guy named James Bryant Conant to whom I'm somehow related. James Bryant Conant was once president of Harvard and also helped develop the atomic bomb, though I usually omit the part about the bomb when I talk about him.

Nashville seems like a place that a Conant could live. Though I never had much experience with the South growing up — didn't know a soul who spoke with a Southern accent, with the exception of funny people in movies — I know that once upon a time many Scotch-Irish moved to the South, and I even heard that country music traces its roots to Irish folk music. But really, Nashville is transplant central: Northerner and Southerner, Australian and Southern Californian, Canadian and Mexican all living hand in hand, side by side, kumbaya. In other words, Nashville is no Grand Rapids. Shawn Mullins says that L.A. is Nashville with a tan, and if there were ever a hip city in flyover country, I think Nashville would be it. I've only been there twice, but I know there are trendy places to hang out in Nashville, places with names like Virago and PM, and I immediately think I might feel cooler if I hung out at place called PM.

Strangely, a Christian publishing company in Nashville is recruiting me — calling after work, e-mailing me — and it all feels very secretive. Just yesterday I had lunch with a silver-haired man carrying a briefcase who suggested we meet a few blocks away from the convention center.

"This industry is a small industry, and I'm just looking out for you," he assured me over the phone days before we met. "We wouldn't want people to see you with me since you're currently working for my competitor." This guy is all about being top secret, and I imagine him with a shoe phone and maybe an umbrella that shoots poisonous darts. But to my disappointment, he wasn't wearing a trench coat and hat when I met him the other day, which I thought would be really cool, but I understand why he wasn't. It's July. We're in Denver. It's 95 degrees.

I'm not quite sure how I feel about the silver-haired man, but I feel I'm wanted, that I'm important. In the past, I've had to beg people to hire me. I got my first newspaper job because I kept calling and showing up in the newsroom. I got my first job out of college because the employer wanted my wife to work there, and they found a position for me so they could hire *her*. But these guys are serious about *me*. Me, Cameron Conant, the five-foot-ten-inch kid who got cut from his high school basketball team but wanted to be an NBA player. Me, Cameron Conant, the kid who failed algebra twice, whose wife left him, who has never made more than $36,000 per year. *Me.* It's as if I have some great talent, but really all I have is a not-so-useful degree in American studies and experience writing for a couple of Midwestern newspapers.

This silver-haired man works for the Evil Empire of the Christian book industry, at least that's how we talk about them in Grand Rapids. They're the Microsoft to our Apple, the Yankees to our Red Sox, the L.A. to our San Francisco, and I worry how my colleagues will react if I move over to "the dark side."

Hope gave this company my name, told them I might be interested in a position there, which led to that clandestine lunch yesterday, a lunch where the silver-haired man extended a folder across the table with a job offer inside. I remember how he pursed his lips, trying not to smile as he waited for me to open the folder. The position being offered was "director of marketing." Yes, "director." It wasn't even the position they were initially hiring for. "We actually increased the salary and title to match your qualifications," the silver-haired man said. "We hope you'll be pleased with the offer."

Pleased? I was ecstatic, though slightly alarmed as well. It was more money than I'd ever made—a lot more. I would live near Hope if I accepted. Everything looked great, but it was all more fun to think about than to actually be confronted with. Now I was facing a real, honest-to-goodness, life-altering decision: Leave everything I knew in Grand Rapids for the Evil Empire in Nashville, where things may or may not work out with Hope, or stay in Grand Rapids, keep the same job, the same friends, the memories of my ex-wife everywhere.

Walking through glass doors and into the convention center, a blast of cold air runs through my sweaty, spiky hair. My stomach growls, which I take as evidence that I'm nervous—nervous about all of it, the job, the girl, the really personal book about my divorce. I scan the landscape for Hope, but all I see are hundreds of faceless people going up and down escalators. I look up at the giant banners hanging from the ceiling and see the enormous head of James Dobson with the headline, "Family Man."

I sigh, walk straight ahead, stand near the escalator, and turn around.

I look back through the windows at the Denver skyline.

I'm twenty-eight.

*

Tonight Hope has a surprise for me: a birthday dinner at a skyscraper restaurant. She looks great and I don't look bad either in khakis and a long-sleeved button-up shirt, the sleeves rolled just recklessly enough to look and keep me cool. "This place is supposed to be really great," Hope says as we walk among the tall buildings of downtown Denver. Actually she says, "This plaaacee is supposed to be reeeaalllly grayyyte."

It's been a hot day and now a steamy summer evening as we enter the glass hotel and take an elevator to the top. Walking into the restaurant, I'm in awe of the view. Through unbroken windows, I see the entire city stretching before us, the expanse of roads and buildings stopped only by mountains. The sun hasn't yet sunk behind the mountains, and light is reflecting every-where — off my watch, off the silverware, off the rimmed spec-tacles of the waiter. Golden rays flood the long restaurant, so much so that sunglasses are almost in order. Hope seems less than impressed with the view, but then again, she's a big-city girl from Nashville and I'm from Jackson, Michigan, where the best restaurant in town overlooks Dr. Dave's Backdoor Pub, which everyone knows is a topless bar.

As Hope sits down, I continue to stand, looking at the city, thinking of the passage in the Bible where the Devil takes Jesus up on a mountain and shows him the kingdoms of the world. And the Devil says, "All of this could be yours. All of it. There's just one catch: Bow down and worship me."

The job, the girl, the money, the new book — it's all there for the taking, I think to myself. And why shouldn't it be? This is my time. In fact, I've been through so much pain that this is clearly God's way of cutting me a little slack. Looking on this beautiful scene — the golden mountains, the golden girl — I think of how opposite it all is to the last few years of my life.

I remember the night I lost it, how Sara, my ex-wife, kept screaming at me. Finally I snapped, kicking the empty cat kennel in her general direction, watching it bounce off the wall. I remember how Sara had tears in her eyes as she picked up our meowing Siamese cat, forced a smile, and then said, "It's okay," stroking the cat's head with her delicate hand. I went to the bathroom, looked in the mirror, and didn't even recognize the person I saw staring back at me, not even after I splashed cold water on my face. I thought that if I had the guts, I would swallow an entire bottle of aspirin.

I also remember one Sunday afternoon in the car when Sara kept yelling at me, telling me what a failure I was, what a disappointment, and I began screaming at her. That day, both hands on the wheel, I called her names that good Christian people don't say, things you might hear in a mafia movie, things that would make you cringe if you heard them. I called her names until I was satisfied that I had crushed her spirit. I called her names until all I could hear was silence, a silence that covers dead things — the same silence I heard the day I walked into our apartment and saw half the furniture gone.

And so today, I want good things: happiness, Hope, a little money for once. It certainly doesn't seem greedy to want these things — not after four years of kicking cat kennels and thoughts of swallowing aspirin. The book of Ecclesiastes says, "Remember your Creator in the days of your youth, before the days of trouble come and the years approach when you will say, 'I find no pleasure in them.'"[2] In my case, the days of trouble came early, but those troubles have now gone, and I find myself in a strange position. I'm twenty-eight and have already lost so much, but now with the book and Hope and the new job offer and thoughts of a new city, I feel young again . . . and yet, strangely, I know that deep down, I am very old.

Solomon, the wisest man ever, implores his reader to "remember your Creator in the days of your youth." And if these are still the days of my youth — which, in a world where many people live well past eighty, I guess they are — I'm not really sure if I'm remembering God or not, or what that even means.

I believe that God is real, that even if I tried to get away from him, I couldn't. Sure, I could travel miles from him in my heart, but in another sense, he's everywhere, and to call for him is as easy, or as difficult, as calling a friend next to me. That's why I always find it strange when I see books about "Finding God," because I can't *not* find him — not when he's in the glow of this restaurant, or in a good-night kiss from Hope, or in the face of a mother cradling her newborn, or even in a room where I've just kicked a cat kennel against the wall and my wife has tears in her eyes and I'm thinking of downing aspirin.

Today, tomorrow, this year, it doesn't matter. I'm just taking the good things offered me, and trying to remember that I don't deserve it, trying to remember that it comes from someone who could take it all away. I just want to be happy for a while. I don't have the energy to wrestle with questions that can't be answered, so I'm taking every good thing as a gift from God. I'm not discerning; I'm just taking.

That's how I felt when Hope asked me to go to Orlando with her and two other couples. It was April and we had been talking on the phone for only two weeks. She had just broken up with her boyfriend, who happened to be a professional skateboarder, the kind of guy you'd see on ESPN2 at 3 a.m. skating some half-pipe in Reno, Nevada. I would always grumble about him. I grumbled because after that magical dinner with Hope in the early spring, the one where we talked about *Casablanca*, the one where she kept blushing, *I* wanted to be with her. I grumbled about him because he drove a new BMW convertible, and I drove a 1998 Mercury Sable. I grumbled about him because he was an athlete, and I always wanted to be.

But only three months ago, Hope told me she had broken up with the skateboarder, had this extra plane ticket to Orlando — one she had originally bought for him. There were two other couples going to Universal Studios, and, well, what did I think? *What did I think?* Despite the fact that Universal Studios was just above hell and the Ripley's Wax Museum in Niagara Falls on my list of most desired places to see, I was excited, my palms sweaty, my heart racing. The catch was we would share a hotel room — just the two of us, two beds, but undoubtedly intimate. Christian friends told me it was a stupid idea. "You hardly know her," they said. "Sounds dangerous," someone else cautioned. "Sure, sure," I acknowledged. "I know it does, but . . ."

It was late May when I boarded a plane with Hope and two young married couples. One of the married couples was Hope's business partner, Angela, and her husband, Justin. The other two were friends from Hope's church. Angela gave me a big hug and said something sweet in her Alabama accent, which I expected, because if Hope liked you, Angela liked you.

It was an evening flight from Nashville to Florida as the three women sat in their own row, playing video poker on $400 phones as the plane cut through the black sky. I sat in a separate row with the men watching *Blazing Saddles* on Justin's laptop. Justin and the other guy, Collin, were laughing, headphones on, but I was in my own world. I kept looking over at Hope, watching her perfectly manicured, long fingernails pressing down on the keypad of her phone as she won video dollars. She would occasionally catch me looking and smile.

I notice her fingernails again tonight as I sit at the table in the golden restaurant and watch Hope take the thick white cloth napkin from the table, unfold it, and place it on her lap. "Here's your birthday card," she says, handing me an envelope. "I also have a gift for you, but you have to come to Nashville to get it."

She smiles in that flirtatious way of hers, and I nearly fall into a trance.

As I take the envelope, she says, "Open it." And of course I do, reading a short paragraph that ends, "With love . . ."

I look up.

"With love," I say, repeating the phrase.

Hope blushes and smiles.

"You know, I think twenty-eight is going to be a really good year," I say matter-of-factly.

Hope reaches across the table, momentarily putting her hand on mine.

"Cameron, I think it's going to be a *great* year."

And as she smiles and nods, I believe her.

CHAPTER 3

A TIME TO LOVE

There is a time for everything, and a season for every activity under the heavens: . . . a time to love.[1]

What am I doing?

It's Friday morning and I'm in the Memphis airport, waiting for my connecting flight to Pensacola, Florida, where Hope and her counselor father will pick me up at the airport and drive me to their family's beach house.

This really isn't like me. After an exhausting week in Denver, running through the never-ending corridors of the Colorado Convention Center, standing next to authors, acting like I'm doing something important when I'm really just watching them talk to some Christian TV personality, I should be relaxing in my apartment in Grand Rapids . . . or heck, even at work.

I'm justifying this spur-of-the-moment trip as "comp time"—vacation time I'm allotted for travel or working after hours, though the most difficult thing I did after hours was attend a wine party last week.

This all happened, me here in Memphis waiting for my connecting flight, because I was in Hope's hotel room moments before she left Denver. It was a Wednesday evening and Hope was about to take a late-night flight from Denver to Pensacola to meet her parents for a vacation. "Come," she said, grasping my arm. "Come with me. Change your flight, Cameron."

"You want me to change my flight back to Grand Rapids? Can I do that?"

I tried. I called an attendant at American Airlines, who informed me that, no, I couldn't change my return flight, and so I told Hope on the phone the next day that I was sorry, but I wasn't sure I could go to Pensacola.

"See if you can find a flight when you get home. I really want you here. It's going to be so *boring* if it's just my family, Cameron. I don't have Internet access here, but I'll see if I can find an Internet café and check on some flights for you later."

That wasn't needed. When I opened the door to my apartment shortly before midnight Thursday, I turned on the computer, found a cheap flight to Pensacola via Memphis, and booked it for 7:30 the next morning.

Now here I am, bleary-eyed, mid-morning Friday, in line for a coffee in Memphis, the first leg of my trip behind me. No one but my mom knows I'm here, though I just text-messaged a coworker this question: "Guess where I am?"

The fact that I even have this cell phone to text-message with is because of Hope.

"You don't have a cell phone?" Hope asked months earlier in disbelief. "*Why*? I mean, who doesn't have a *cell phone*?"

"Me, I guess."

I tried to play it off as an aversion to cell phones, but I really just wanted to save money—something a girl who drove a

Hummer probably wouldn't understand. I mean, after all, she already knew that I drove a Mercury Sable, and I didn't want to do any more damage to my hip quotient.

Hope once said, "Cameron, you're not a things person," and I liked that, but I never wanted to embarrass her because of the car I drove, or the cell phone I didn't have, or the money I refused to spend. In addition to saving money, another reason I didn't have a cell phone was that I had so few people wanting to contact me. Most of my friends had disappeared during my marriage, which made the divorce all the more difficult . . . and finding Hope all the more incredible.

Hope was strong medicine for my loneliness and flagging confidence, even if hanging out with her did mean spending money on cell phones and last-minute trips to Pensacola and expensive dinners. After a while, I felt like the guy who wondered how he ever got through the day without a couple of Vicodin, or how he ever got to sleep without a sedative.

After her comment about me not having a cell phone, I asked Hope which carrier she used, and two weeks later, I found myself in a Sprint store, selecting the high-usage plan. I did other strange things too, like download AOL Instant Messenger — something I once thought only high school kids used — because Hope used it. Late at night, Hope and I would have conversations over Instant Messenger, one of which went like this:

HOPEinNASHVILLE: Hey
CAMERON7117: How are you?
HOPEinNASHVILLE: Fine . . . you should come to Nashville
CAMERON7117: Or you to Grand Rapids . . .
HOPEinNASHVILLE: Cameron, people don't move from Nashville to Grand Rapids. Why don't you come and visit me

this weekend? Come after work on Friday. Or just take Friday off and come. Yay! Come and visit me!

I did. I drove nine hours from Michigan to Nashville, arriving at her house at 3 a.m. "Well, guess where I'm headed?" I asked my mom from my new cell phone, headed south through Indiana.

"Tennessee?"

I remember Hope calling me at least five times that night: 7 p.m.: "Have you left? Where are you?" 9 p.m.: "Hi, just checking up on you." 11 p.m.: "So let me tell you something funny." 1 a.m.: "When are you getting here?" 1:45 a.m.: "I'm on the couch. Call me when you get here. I'm watching a movie." I rolled in just before 3 a.m., parking in front of her *Truman Show* house — two stories, front porch, white shutters, hanging flowers. Hope stumbled to the door in a pink bathrobe, eyes half-open. She hugged me and proceeded to show me to the guest room upstairs. After using the bathroom, I climbed into bed and saw that I had, of all things, a text message from Hope, downstairs.

I looked at my glowing phone in the dark room.

"Glad you're here."

Hope's dad is tall with a long, bony face, spectacles, and thinning gray hair. I'd met him once before, and when I did, he had a deliberate, slow way of speaking — sort of what you'd expect from a counselor — and a pleasant Southern accent. I now see him for the second time ever, this time sitting behind the wheel of a beige SUV outside the airport in Pensacola, his daughter in the front seat next to him. They are stuck behind a long line of cars, all trying to pull curbside where dozens of people like me stand with suitcases, covered by the overhang on this rainy, humid day.

They finally pull up, Hope changes seats, and five minutes later I hear Hope saying, "Dad, do you want coffee?" He says nothing for at least ten seconds and then in a flat tone responds, "No, not really." Another ten seconds pass and Hope says, "I'd like coffee. Let's stop." Hope is definitely daddy's little girl, and, well, next thing I know, we're pulling into the Starbucks parking lot.

Back in the car, Hope and I talk about funny things we saw at the book convention in Denver, the people we know, the inside jokes we have from the show, like the one about the carved wooden manger scene displayed in the back of a red convertible.

"Why was a manger scene in a convertible? I just don't get it," I say, smiling. Hope laughs. "I have no idea. It was just strange."

It was strange when Hope suggested we buy a six-pack of Corona hours later and hide it under the stilted beach house so her parents wouldn't see us drinking. "Would drinking Corona upset them?" I ask. Hope shrugs her shoulders. "They're just weird like that," she says. The day is now blue as we lie on a hammock underneath the stilted house, a breeze gently blowing, sunlight spilling through the boards above us. Two opened Coronas are twisted into the sand, and the four remaining bottles are wrapped in a paper bag, hidden behind a garbage can.

Hope is reading a Donald Miller book and suggests we read together, and I agree. I agree even though I remember how Hope had coffee with Donald Miller recently, how she raves about him all the time, how it sort of annoys me, and this is what I'm thinking every time she says the name Donald Miller. The book is called *Searching for God Knows What*, and even I have to admit that it's a great title and that Donald Miller writes really

interesting books, though me being small and selfish as I sometimes am, I wish *I* had written those really interesting books.
But because I fear imitating a fellow memoirist—yes, I'm now
a memoirist, I tell myself—and because I am sometimes very
small, I never read much of Donald Miller's stuff.

Hope asks me to read the third chapter aloud, and as I do, I
hear my voice giving shape to the words, feel Hope lying next to
me on the hammock, her right arm and leg touching mine, and
I realize that I'm comprehending only about 1 percent of what
I'm reading. If I had to guess, I'd say that I'm comprehending
only about 1 percent of my life, too—me, the divorced guy on a
hammock in Pensacola trying to hide my insecurities lying next
to a gorgeous woman trying to hide Corona from her parents.

Insecurities, you ask? Here's what's going through my head:
*I love you, Hope. I'm terrified you won't love me back. I'm terrified
you'll leave me just like Sara did. I'm terrified I'll move to Nashville
and you'll forget about me. I'm terrified your parents won't love me
as much as I want them to. Don't you know how wounded I am?
Don't you know how much it meant the night you said my ex-wife
was crazy? Crazy for reacting the way she did, crazy for not wanting me? Don't you know how I felt when we held each other on
the couch that weekend I visited you in Nashville—the night we
watched* The Last Samurai *and you almost fell asleep in my arms?
Don't you know what it did to me when you made me dinner in
your house at the glass kitchen table, the jazz music, the candles, the
way you asked if I wanted any more to eat?*

I say none of this, of course, but just keep reading words
from *Searching for God Knows What*. Hope puts her chin on my
neck, and I hear waves from the Gulf of Mexico, only fifty yards
behind us, rolling into shore.

*

"So, Cameron, what are you going to do about this job offer in Nashville?" Hope's mom asks at the restaurant, my second night in Pensacola. She's short and stocky and wonderful—a strong Christian woman who, like me, wouldn't shy away from telling a slightly bawdy story or, unlike me, wouldn't think twice about giving Hope a piece of her mind. She's also the sort of person who would do anything for anyone—would give you a place to live if you didn't have one, or an encouraging word if you needed to hear it.

She's the epitome of Southern—wears makeup to the grocery store and makes okra and tells stories about a pet pig that almost attacked her—yet she's big on manners and decorum and Bless her Hearts, which in the South means you're about to say something you might feel guilty about. She's a woman I would love to have as a mother-in-law.

But tonight her frank question catches me off guard, though I suppose it shouldn't because I know some of the blunt things she's asked Hope before. We're on a wooden porch, multi-colored Christmas lights dangling above us, a view of the harbor. Like most of the restaurants in the area, the food is mostly fried, comes in baskets, and tastes like Chicken McNuggets without the chicken. It's just Hope and me along with her mom and her spectacle-clad father at the table tonight, even though Hope's older brother and his wife are in town.

"Well, I don't know," I say, trying not to call her Carol, though that's her first name and she's told me to call her that. "I guess I'm not really sure. It would be tough to leave Grand Rapids—all of my friends there, a great company, but maybe it's time for a change. I really like Nashville."

We're all thinking the same thing, but no one's saying it, not even Hope's mom. We're thinking this: Of course Cameron will move to Nashville. He loves Hope; Nashville's a great city; he's being offered a lot of money. Why wouldn't he move? Hope's parents have seen this all before, most notably with Kevin, who was not from Michigan or Ohio or California or even Hawaii. No, frosted-haired Kevin was from New Zealand, a good twenty-four-hour flight away from Nashville. Kevin and Hope started talking, and Kevin must've fallen into the same trance I did, because only a beautiful woman could make someone leave one of the most beautiful places on earth for a landlocked city in middle America.

Hope recently learned that Kevin is now married, and she sounded surprised when she heard it, and then laughed, though I think it might have hurt her because the laugh had a mournful sound to it, the sort of laugh you give when you're too tired or embarrassed to cry. Hope has nothing but good things to say about Kevin, and last night we watched a Kiwi movie that he introduced Hope's family to last year. Everyone loved the movie, and I guess Hope's mom is instituting a new family tradition of watching it each year in Pensacola. As the popcorn popped and Hope's parents found their places in front of the TV, I started moping around, acting like a baby.

I didn't want to watch Kevin's movie.

And then Hope said something I'm still thinking of today: "Cameron, we don't act like things didn't happen."

I guess that's something a therapist's daughter *would* say, but I thought it was really good, the whole idea of being transparent, of acknowledging the past but not wallowing in it, of enjoying the movie the ex-boyfriend introduced you to even if the ex-boyfriend wasn't around anymore. I stopped moping around after that, even though I was still afraid of becoming Kevin, being replaced by another more interesting guy a year later.

*

Hope and I walk along the water the next day, where we see kids kneeling on a bridge looking at catfish. Some of them join the catfish in the water, squealing as they jump. "So what are you going to do, Cameron?" Hope asks, her voice sounding like a twenty-seven-year-old version of her mother's. She knows I have only one week to make my decision about Nashville and the new job. "I just want you to know that whatever you do, don't make this decision for me. You do what is best for you. Take me out of the equation."

Of course her request is impossible, though I appreciate the sentiment. Or do I? No, maybe I don't. I really want her to say, "Cameron, whatever you do, please come to Nashville. I love you. I need you there." She doesn't say that, and part of me wonders if she's saying what she needs to say in order to wash her hands of the matter, knowing she'll discard me as soon as I move to Nashville.

I feel as if I'm being drawn to Nashville, a pull I have no control over, but part of me resists the pull, like the guy in a movie who clings to the edge of a building even though it's clear that his fingers will soon give way to gravity. The situation I'm falling into isn't ideal. Hope and I both know the company offering me a job might be a difficult place to work. And this weighs on me, keeping me in that itchy, dry place of indecision.

But then Hope says, "I mean . . . do you really want to stay in Grand Rapids?"

I stare at the water, the kids jumping. I hear their splashes, their squeals. My eyes glaze over, the sun beating down on my bare shoulders. I am quiet and still.

"No," I finally say, looking quizzically at Hope, surprised by my answer. "No, I don't."

Hope smiles, kisses me on the lips, and puts her arms around me.

She knows I've made my decision.

*

I'm back in my apartment in Grand Rapids, standing next to one of the white walls where a picture once hung. My wife took it when she left, and the area the picture once covered is now brighter than the rest of the wall. I'm holding my cell phone, watching my fingers dial the number I've been dreading to call. I hear a voice on the other end. It's the silver-haired man.

"Hello, Michael? It's Cameron."

"Helloooo, Cameron."

It's 6:15 p.m. and it sounds as if Michael, the silver-haired man, is in the car, driving. "So, how was your day?" I ask to be polite.

"Well, anytime the CEO pats you on the back and says, 'Boy, I'm glad we have you on our team,' I'd say it's a pretty good day," Michael says, hardly restraining his glee. "I gave a presentation today on some pretty innovative marketing concepts, and the presentation went really well. If you come on board, I'll be able to tell you more."

"Well, actually that's what I'm calling about," I say, a lump in my throat. "I'm calling to accept your offer."

Michael lets out a "Woo-hoo!" and laughs and says his day has just gotten better. He tells me to call his secretary tomorrow, that they'll pay for my moving expenses, just to get a couple of rate quotes first. "Oh, and Cameron, I want you to be prepared for something: When you tell them you're leaving tomorrow, they're going to walk you out of the building, but you walk out with your head held high. You've done nothing wrong. You're just taking a better opportunity."

I hang up the phone and feel sick to my stomach. I hate thinking of what my boss's reaction will be tomorrow. My boss who one day gave me three energy drinks and laughed as I drank them all. My boss who always asked what projects I wanted to work on, and what did I think of this or that, and thanks for your good work, Cameron. I'd have to tell him I was leaving for our publishing rival in Nashville, despite the fact that the people at the company in Grand Rapids put their hands on my shoulders and looked me in the eye, and laughed at my jokes, and told me how lucky they were to have me.

But I was doing this for Hope, I told myself. When we tried to have a "define the relationship" conversation once, Hope said, "Well, we can't really date if we're not in the same city, can we? I don't think so." I told her we could, but she said she'd done that before, that it didn't work, that we had to be in the same city, and, well, "people don't move from Nashville to Michigan."

I didn't tell Michael my true motives for taking this job, not even when he asked me point-blank over the phone why I wanted it. That's probably one of the many reasons I'm not at peace with this decision, but that's not what I tell my parents or close friends. "I just feel a lot of peace about this," I say. "Just a lot of peace." It's nonsense. I feel peace like there was peace after we dropped the atomic bomb on Japan, the bomb my relative James Bryant Conant helped perfect.

I too had to annihilate the opposition, silence the internal voices that told me this decision was crazy. And so I did, convincing myself that I was just being a baby—afraid to make a decision, take a risk. Anytime I'm afraid to risk, I'd rather force a jump than sit still.

Today, I jumped. I call Hope minutes after I hang up with Michael and recount the conversation, his reaction. She laughs, puts the phone below her mouth, and says, "Hey, Mom, Michael yelled 'Woo-hoo.'"

I smile and laugh uneasily.

*

I just moved to Nashville a week ago and my furniture has yet to arrive. Leaving Grand Rapids was difficult. After I told my boss I was leaving, I handed him a typed letter at 4:45 p.m. and left for the day. He was shocked. "I'm not sure what to say," he stammered. "I didn't expect this—you going to our biggest competitor. I'm not sure this has ever happened, but I think we'll let you stay for two more weeks, maybe longer if you'd agree to that. I'm short-staffed already." It was 5 p.m. when I got in my car, but one hour later, human resources called me, said not to come back, that I was done, hoped I understood, and so I never had those last two weeks to say good-bye.

A friend called me and said she couldn't understand how I was leaving for *that* company. "What are you thinking?" she asked. She said I was a traitor. She actually called me a traitor. Another friend left a voice mail begging me to reconsider, imploring me to see if Grand Rapids would take me back.

Almost three weeks later, I'm in Tennessee ahead of my furniture, which is in a warehouse somewhere waiting to be loaded onto a truck. Instead of sitting on the floor leaning against a white wall, in a room with only a clock radio, a couple bags of clothes, and a basket with Nashville maps and a bottle of wine, I'm spending Saturday at a bookstore in Franklin, a wealthy suburb of Nashville. I'm currently in the bookstore café, facing a man in a cowboy hat sipping coffee from across the room, a guitar case at his feet.

I feel as if I'm in a daze. It was only last night that Hope threw a "Welcome to Nashville" party for me. Hope's parents were there along with Angela and Justin. We had dinner at a small Italian restaurant and sat on the porch, the humid August evening filled with laughter. Justin paid for my dinner, Hope's parents gave me a restaurant gift certificate, and at the end of the night, Hope and I left together in her car.

As we drove down the dark street, we were both silent. "Are you okay?" I asked, wondering why she wasn't happier on such a festive evening, an evening I had been looking forward to since Hope first told me about the party two weeks ago. I ask if she's okay because of the way she reluctantly held my hand all night.

"I'm just having a PMS day, Cameron. It's nothing."

Silence.

"I think there's something else," I said.

I waited.

"You need to know that just because you're here now doesn't mean I'm ready to start dating you," Hope said.

Are you kidding? I thought to myself. *What did I need to do for this girl? What had I done, moving to this place? Why was I such an idiot, loving her like I did? Was this worth it, me forever not knowing where we stood?* I'm still thinking these things now as I watch the cowboy drink his coffee and talk to a woman who just sat down.

I get up, down the last few sips, and walk past the cowboy, past aisles of hardcovers and paperbacks and best sellers and local authors, and I wonder if I could ever get my book on the local-authors shelf, now that I'm local. I pick up a Lauren Winner book and read a few paragraphs. It's good, really good, and I'm immediately depressed. *Why can't I write like that? I can't. I can't write like that*, I think. I would normally be inspired to go and write something after reading such clean prose, but I know that I won't, not today. Today I feel like a refugee. *Where should I go now*, I wonder, and for some reason I think, *the mall*—perhaps because it's the only place in town I can find without a map.

Fifteen minutes later I'm standing near Dillard's, wondering why it seems as if everyone is walking hand in hand. I take the escalator to the second floor and walk by another bookstore, and this time, I notice the magazines—beautiful, half-naked women draped across the covers—and I remember how my wife saw me glancing at an issue of *Maxim* one night in a bookstore café. I glanced not just because of my libido, but because I felt so alone. I imagined that beautiful woman on the cover looking at me, wanting me. Only me.

Later that night in our apartment, after my wife saw me staring at the photo, she made accusations about lust, masturbation, cheating, telling me I was a pervert, that I never touched her because I was too busy touching myself. She told me that I was forever dreaming about touching other women and that Jesus had said in his Sermon on the Mount that if you lust after another woman, it's the same as adultery, which made me an adulterer. I guess that's why she left that night, because who would want to sleep next to an adulterer? That night, through the kitchen window, I watched Sara's taillights disappear. And though she returned a day later, she never really came back.

Today I look at a row of men's magazines and feel sad knowing that men like me are drawn to the women on the covers. I feel sad knowing that some women feel valued only when men stare at their breasts or butt or legs, and yet, some guy will get in a relationship with a cover model and will never want her to dress like she does in the magazine. He will never want other men to look at her the way he once did.

My whole life feels like it's falling apart. Is this what I get for loving, for caring for someone? I get "Just because you moved here doesn't mean I'm ready to start dating"? I turn on my cell phone as I walk out of the mall and see that Hope still hasn't called or text-messaged. It's 4:30 p.m. She knows I have none of my furniture, know virtually no one, have nothing to do, that I don't start work for another few days, and still, nothing.

I go back to my empty apartment, which feels like a Bedouin tent on this ninety-degree day, and turn on the air conditioning. I open the bottle of red wine Hope gave me and pour myself a glass, sitting on the beige carpet, back against the wall. It's about 5 p.m., no word from Hope, and I have an entire evening to kill. I consider going to a movie by myself, but the only thing I know that's playing is *Dukes of Hazzard*, and I'd rather sit here with my wine than go watch *Dukes of Hazzard*. After my second glass of wine, I text-message a beautiful girl with long legs, Caroline, who I met at a work orientation the other day. We exchanged phone numbers, and I say in my text message, "We should do something sometime." Then, like a desperate fifteen-year-old trying to make the popular girl jealous, I text-message Hope: "I just asked Caroline, the girl from work, out. Hope you don't mind."

I know this will lead to some sort of confrontation, which is exactly why I do it. War is better than apathy. Soon Hope is standing at the door to my apartment and we're yelling at each other. "This is really mature, Cameron. Well, go. Go ahead and go out with Caroline. Do whatever you want." "Fine, I will!" I say, feeling the three glasses of wine I've just had. "You're ridiculous," she says, and I say, "You're ridiculous." She yells that she's leaving and doesn't know when or if she'll talk to me again, and I yell, "Fine, go, just go!" and make a sweeping motion with my hand. She follows the motion, and leaves.

As I slam the door I have a sinking feeling I've just destroyed the only beautiful thing in my life, and maybe I have, which leads me to do something I've never done before: drink an entire bottle of wine in one sitting. An hour later, I take the last few sips, finishing the bottle off. I realize how my face feels soft and relaxed and tingly. I think of Caroline and her long legs. I think of the curves on the twenty-five-year-old woman in the rental office, the one who is always so attentive when I ask her a question about my apartment. I think of anything other than Hope.

Four days later I'm preparing dinner when I hear a knock. I haven't heard from Hope since our shouting match, but here she is in the doorway, holding flowers, of all things. Her eyes are soft and gentle. "I'm sorry," she says. I take the flowers and give her a hug. We say nothing for half a minute, stuck in the embrace. Five minutes later, we're sitting on the floor, my furniture still ten days from arriving, and Hope says, "You have to understand where I'm at. Of course I like you, Cameron, I just need you to give me time . . . let me go at my own pace."

Three weeks later, I'm tired of letting Hope go at her own pace. She told me to listen to a song recently with melancholy lyrics, and I had no idea what the song was supposed to mean or if the lyrics were meant for me. The song was about wanting to love someone but always disconnecting when they got too close. The singer kept repeating the word "disconnect."

I listen to that song as I drive to Hope's. I've just gotten out of a meeting and I'm leaving work early and headed to her *Truman Show* house with the hanging flowers and white shutters and gazebo in back. She usually sits with her laptop and her big white dog on the couch next to her — a dog that is stubborn and needy and runs away if there's a crack in the gate. This always makes Hope cry and she spends the next five hours putting up posters and then someone finds the dog in a supermarket parking lot and she's happy and goes to bed early. As I drive, I pray, *God, give me the words to say and the strength to say them. And if you don't want me to say these things, let me know somehow.*

I'm planning to say that I love her too much to keep spinning my wheels in a relationship that she's afraid to even call a relationship. I'm planning to say that I didn't sign up for a friendship, especially one in which we kiss and go to romantic dinners and e-mail seven times a day and talk on the phone at least twice. I'm planning to say that I never want to see her again.

I open the front door, and she hears me and yells that she's in the back. I walk through the kitchen and see her to the right, in her bedroom, still in her pajamas, lying in bed with her laptop. "I'm being lazy today," she says, smiling that smile that the youngest kids in any family are famous for — the sort of smile that says, "I'm the baby and I know I'm adorable and I know you think so too." And I do. Hope has an older brother who used to get into a lot of trouble — did things like tap neighbors' phone lines and detonate small bombs in the driveway — but Hope was sort of the crown jewel of the family, the sweet one, the one who didn't rock the boat. The baby.

As I sit in an armchair in her room, she sits up in bed and her expression changes from bemused to serious. She knows something's wrong, could tell the moment I walked into the room. I sit there rigidly and close my eyes. "Hope, you know I really care about you," I say, now opening my eyes. She nods, her mouth frowning, her brow furrowed. "But I can't keep doing this. I can't keep seeing you like this when we're not even dating . . . I can't force you to be in a place you're not, but I'm not willing to do what we're doing now . . ." Hope looks horrified, and I see her gulp and readjust her legs on the bed.

"Do you remember that question I asked you one time? 'If you could take one person with you to a deserted island, who would you take?' You never asked me what I thought, but if you had, I would've said, 'You. I choose you.'"

I think to myself, *Wow, that sounded like a line out of a movie*, and then I see Hope crying, and I think, *Yes, this would happen in the movie too.*

She cries and says, "I just want to be so careful. I just want to make sure we're both ready to date. I want to be with you." Suddenly, I'm getting emotion from her I've rarely seen, and my concerns melt away. I'm still not quite myself, my shoulders are still tense, but we hug, and when I leave, I can tell that Hope is different, worried. I can tell that she realizes something about me that she hadn't before.

*

It's late September and Hope and I are near Dallas, Texas, for a wedding. A college friend of hers is getting married, and Hope is one of about twelve bridesmaids, which seems weird, but maybe it's just a Southern thing.

I'm sitting in a church pew watching Hope and an army of women await instructions from the wedding coordinator, a tall gray-haired woman in her late fifties with a long nose and a bullhorn. Hope occasionally smiles and whispers something to a friend, and they try not to laugh because you don't want to laugh when there's a woman with a bullhorn. I see other men around me, arms extended along the tops of the pews. Some of the men have cameras around their necks, while others play with cell phones or crane their heads back, staring at the ceiling fans. I'm happy to be among their ranks, watching the beautiful women, happy to know that one of them is with me.

I'm also happy to say that the conversation in Hope's bedroom, the one where I told her I couldn't live with the ambiguity anymore, seems decades ago, even though it was only last month. It seems decades ago because two weeks later Hope was standing in a parking lot, kissing me, telling me she'd like to be my girlfriend. She brought me coffee that day, and I walked back to my office, smiling, drinking the coffee, while Hope drove away, smiling, calling people and telling them we were dating. She told people this the way some women might announce an engagement.

I watch the soon-to-be-married couple talking to the pastor, and I look back at the army of women behind them, all college friends from Kansas. And all married.

But one.

"So are you next, Hope? Will we all get together next year for *your* wedding?" someone asked earlier in the parking lot. Hope smiled. "I don't know. We'll see."

Somehow, Hope has gone from undecided, distant, and irritable, to explaining the type of engagement ring she'd like — the sort of cut, the setting, everything. Ever since our bedroom conversation, Hope has been saying, "I've never felt like this about someone," and, "Is this crazy, Cameron, us talking about marriage? I don't know." I don't know either, but I do know that as I see her now, looking like a senator's wife or heiress to a small kingdom in the south of France, I wonder what my ex-wife would think of this.

A week before I moved to Nashville, I talked to Sara for three hours on the phone. It was only the second time we had spoken since she left, and I called to tell her things, things about how I forgave her and how I hoped she forgave me. "Hey, it's Cameron," I said as she picked up the phone. "You probably didn't expect to hear from *me*," I added, laughing nervously.

But despite all that forgiveness, there was and still is this darkness inside of me, this need to prove her wrong, to show her how stupid she was for leaving.

Look at me, Sara, I want to say, *look at me sitting here in a church pew in Texas, my beautiful girlfriend, maybe one of the most beautiful women in the world—intelligent, regal—standing next to all of these other intelligent, beautiful women.*

I want her to see all of these things, as if that would make anything better, as if that would remove the scar on my heart.

In the book of Ecclesiastes, Solomon writes that there is a time for everything under heaven, including a time to love, and today, it feels good to love. I did very little of this in my marriage. I loved Sara, but I wonder if too often that love was swallowed by resentment. But now is my time to love, to love unselfishly, to give myself to another person. The Scriptures say that God is love, and so wherever we see love, we see God. But do people see God when they see me interact with Hope? Or do they see neediness, desperation, a drowning man clinging to a piece of driftwood?

I think of these things the next day. The wedding is over and Hope and I are driving to Dallas to drink wine with the bridal party. In the car Hope plays an Eva Cassidy ballad called "Songbird," which she says would make a good wedding song.

We squeeze hands and drive straight into the orange sun, which melts into the flat beige landscape. And as we hold hands, the music still playing, I think of how my friends are wrong about us. My cautious friends tense up and tighten their lips and nod slowly when I describe my roller-coaster relationship with Hope. Maybe they think we are too combustible together, or maybe they see me as a drowning man clinging to a piece of driftwood, thinking Hope will be my salvation.

And maybe I am drowning.
And maybe I do think she'll be my salvation.
And maybe she could be.

CHAPTER 4

A TIME TO HATE

There is a time for everything, and a season for every activity under the heavens: . . . a time to hate.[1]

Driving to work this morning, five minutes from my office, I suddenly realize that I'm supposed to be at a hotel for a meeting. It's gray outside and I speed up and switch lanes because I can't be late today—not when important people will turn around and stare at me if I walk in past 8:30. It's 8:15 as I veer into the carpool lane, though I shouldn't because I'm the only passenger in the car and I could get pulled over for this sort of thing.

With one eye on the road, I rummage through a pile of CDs, searching for U2's rendition of the Elvis song "I Can't Help Falling in Love with You." The U2 rendition is moody and gray, perfect for a day like this, and it's become one of my favorites since moving to Nashville. November in Nashville is sunny compared to Michigan, but today is an "I Can't Help Falling in Love with You" kind of day, though tomorrow might just be a "Mysterious Ways" sort of a day. I'll just have to see what the weather is like.

Sunny or cloudy, U2 always seems to say the right thing, which is why I can't help but talk about the band when the opportunity arises. Give me a minute and I'll tell you how The Edge, U2's lead guitarist and backup vocalist, is a philosopher with a guitar, or Bono, a theologian with a microphone. I titled my first book *With or Without You* because it's the name of one of U2's biggest hits. Some people might think it's lame that I did that, and maybe it is, but U2 got me through my dark night of the soul, my divorce, and for that I am grateful. I should really say that God got me through the divorce, and he did, but I've found that God almost always uses messengers.

Bono was my messenger.

God's messengers are often unlikely people, people like John the Baptist, a wild-eyed evangelist who lived in the desert and ate locusts and honey, or King Solomon, who had more wives than some countries have soldiers, or Bono, lead singer of an Irish rock band who sometimes drinks too much but is always tackling poverty and AIDS and trying to live out that part of the Lord's Prayer where Jesus talks about bringing heaven on earth.

Bono, like Solomon, admits his penchant for hypocrisy, which I appreciate. "I don't believe in riches, but you should see where I live," Bono sings, and I know where he lives: an Irish mansion, a Manhattan penthouse, a beach house on the Mediterranean. But, ah, Bono, I could say things like that too. "I don't believe in selfishness, but you should see how I live." Hope gets me high like a drug, and I selfishly want more and more of her to the exclusion of almost everything else. I say I want to help others, but really I just want to get over to Hope's house and look into her eyes and kiss her full lips.

I never really knew much about U2 until my divorce, but after Sara left, it was all I could listen to. I remember standing in the bathroom mirror listening to the song "All Because of You" on my iPod, screaming the line, "I'm not broke but you can see the cracks. You can make me perfect again." There was something cathartic about standing in the bathroom mirror, screaming, "I'm not broke but you can see the cracks." I knew how The Edge had gone through a divorce and how that, on some level, influenced an album called *Achtung Baby*. Albums like *Achtung Baby* introduced me to a God I never knew — a God of second chances and to people who were guilty and wounded but forgiven and reaching for something better.

Grace, this idea of getting what we don't deserve, appeals to me, probably because I remember having visions of antigrace, of sitting in church as a teenager and imagining all of the bad things I had ever done projected onto the screen, the one behind the pastor, the one where all the song lyrics appeared each Sunday. I imagined how horrified the congregation would be if they knew how I stared at the beautiful brown-haired girl every week and undressed her with my eyes while the pastor talked about sin or atonement.

I guess in those days, the God I knew was ready to pounce on me. He was making a list and checking it twice — not a God of second chances, but a God of "You had your chance but you blew it." But then I came across U2, believers who admitted they were messed up but wanted to be better, believers who sang "Hallelujah" at the end of their concerts, Bono on his knees, many fans not understanding what was happening. Believers who could sing things like, "I have held the hand of the devil. It was warm in the night. I was cold as a stone." I knew exactly what U2 meant. And so would most of the people in the Bible, come to think of it.

The Christianity I knew was all about having the right answers, but I now prefer those who minister out of weakness to those who minister out of a "look how much I know" attitude. I see U2 ministering out of weakness, even if Bono does wear fly shades and strut onstage, if only to mock his own celebrity.

So imagine how I felt when my boss handed me a folded piece of paper three hours after I arrived this morning and said, "Have a good time." Standing in a hotel conference room, I took the piece of paper from his hand, stepped into the lobby, and read, "Get in the car. I'm outside. We're going to see U2 in St. Louis as an early Christmas present. Love, Hope." I walked into the now misty November day and saw Hope at the wheel of my silver Mazda 3, which I bought just before I moved to Nashville, a black bag in the back with clothes stuffed in it. I have no idea how she pulled this off; I just know that I'm now driving with my hand in hers, and she's looking at me, smiling, saying, "Are you surprised?"

I quote Clark Griswold from the movie *Christmas Vacation*: "I wouldn't be any more surprised if I woke up with my face sewn to the carpet." Hours later, we're in rural Illinois, black sky, and I'm going a hundred miles per hour. "I think we'll be okay," I say after an unexpected thirty-minute detour, one in which I took a wrong turn. "I think we'll make it on time."

We do. Arriving at our hotel—a historic, converted train station in downtown St. Louis—we throw our bags in the room and walk a few chilly blocks to the arena, where we find our seats with twenty minutes to spare. Hope is holding a beer and eating nachos with orange cheese, and I'm trying to let this whirlwind day sink in. I'm at a U2 concert, my first ever, yet all I can think about is how my relationship with Hope feels as if it's on the verge of a meltdown.

As we approached St. Louis, Hope told me about this guy who kept contacting her through MySpace, but she was just shrugging him off, not responding to his messages. But the way she talked about it made me uneasy and jealous. Maybe I wouldn't have been uneasy if Hope had shown some interest in kissing me once in a while, but she hadn't. We had also been squabbling, having stupid arguments that made no sense.

One argument happened two weeks ago. Hope, Angela, Justin, and I were going to dinner and I couldn't find my way to the restaurant, a restaurant I'd been to only hours before. The fact is, I couldn't find my way out of a cardboard box, and Hope hated this about me. But being a people pleaser, not wanting Hope to dislike *anything* about me, I started getting frustrated that I couldn't find the restaurant. Hope was in the front seat next to me, Angela and Justin in back.

"I know I'm close to the restaurant, but is it up here?" I asked, pointing to a strip mall. I heard giggling in the back and Hope smiled, bit her bottom lip, and pointed, and I turned the steering wheel in that direction. Soon, I was driving through a dark parking lot, asking if this was it, my face red. The laughter was getting louder, and Hope bit her lip harder, smirking, saying, "Up here," pointing to an adjacent strip mall. I knew I was being laughed at, felt beads of sweat forming on my forehead, but I did as she said. Soon the entire car erupted in laughter. "Don't you know where it is? You were just there!" they said, and I said, "No, I don't, seriously, where is it? All these strip malls look the same. I'm not very good with directions."

I was angry, embarrassed, hurt, and they were laughing.

Hope and I had it out later, me leaning against the car, telling her how hurt I was, asking why she pointed the wrong direction and laughed, her telling me how frustrated she was. "I guess my dad just always takes care of everything. I never have to worry how to get somewhere—he always knows how to get there. But with you, it's frustrating."

My inability to find restaurants is one of the smaller things Hope dislikes about me. She also dislikes how she always has to plan our evenings, or days, or weekends. She's the local girl who knows all of the places to go, and I, the out-of-towner who allows her to sweep me into her tornado. But Hope likes it when someone takes charge or even challenges her, which is why she reacted so positively to that conversation in her bedroom two months ago—the one where I told her I didn't know if I could spend time with her anymore.

But that was the exception. Most of the time, I feel weak, acting out scenes from my dysfunctional marriage. "People don't move to Michigan, Cameron, they move to Nashville," Hope had said before I moved, her tornado swirling. My answer: "Right, I know, I know."

The week at Universal Studios when Hope and I hardly knew each other, we watched an episode of *Storm Stories* on the Weather Channel from our separate twin beds. Hope was familiar with tornados, remembers one during her college days that tore up the town, and ironically the very storm she remembers was the focus of that episode of *Storm Stories*.

It was dark in our hotel room, the only light the flicker of the television set, when Hope told me the story. She said she was processing photos in the darkroom of the art building when all hell broke loose, and she heard sirens and was afraid to leave. She ducked under a desk and prayed everything would be okay. But everything wasn't okay. Dozens of people died, and the next day, Hope went downtown with her camera, photographing neighborhoods that looked like war zones.

One week later, she was in that same darkroom, processing black-and-white photos of strewn metal and homeless cats. That's why Hope cringed and hid under covers as they showed footage of the storm — the storm that could've killed her, the storm she had no power over — and I remember thinking, *I know how you feel*. I feel as if I have no power over this relationship, that I care too much and am still so wounded from the divorce, so needy, and I hate that I feel this way.

I look at Hope, the lights dimming, the crowd now roaring in the auditorium, and I clutch her hand and look into her eyes. They look empty and hollow. I'm looking right through her, and as I do, I remember that night I touched her, lying beneath her. I remember how she liked the way I touched her but then pulled back because she said it was too much, and why wasn't I respecting her, and I felt dirty and ashamed because she was right. And then it happened again, us kissing on the bed, me getting carried away, touching her, and then her saying I wasn't respecting her.

"Just like so many other guys I've dated, I don't feel I can trust being physical with you," she would say after that, and her words reminded me of my ex-wife who had said something similar, and suddenly it didn't seem so crazy that Sara — or now, maybe even Hope — thought I was a pervert. And so there would be no more kissing passionately — at least that's the impression I get when she says things like, "I'm just not there yet, and I don't know when I will be" after a particularly uninspired kiss. I'm not looking through Hope now but through Bono who's preening on stage. And he's singing "I Still Haven't Found What I'm Looking For."

*

I bought my mom some $50 towels once, but I'm not sure I've spent that much on a gift since then, and yet here I am in a furniture store, staring at two chairs that will set me back $1,200. It's December 15 and I'm scheduled to fly home to Michigan in a week, which means I need to get Hope something for Christmas before I leave. She recently bought a second house and needs to fill it with stuff, primarily stuff to sit on, which is why I'm looking at two "Edinburgh chairs" for the ends of her antique dining room table. The chairs have arms and are made of dark wood. I'm looking at them because Hope said she wanted to put an eclectic mix of chairs at the table, so I thought these could be the cornerstone chairs and she could put others around them.

Maybe if I buy her the chairs, she'll be happy and will see how much I care about her, because if I didn't care, what am I doing spending over $1,000 on a Christmas gift? As I walk to the cash register, I swallow hard and remind myself how much she'll like the chairs, what her face will look like when they're delivered next week. But then I learn that the chairs won't be delivered until February. "We don't have any in the warehouse and I can't sell the floor models," the sales associate says, shaking her head. I hesitate for a moment, but then she says the word "Polaroid," and I pull out my credit card.

I carry a Polaroid photo of the chairs into Hope's house a week later. It's December 22 and I fly to Michigan tomorrow, so Hope and I are giving each other gifts. We're in the bedroom of her new house, a house she bought two months ago when I was looking for a place. Hope encouraged me to buy a home, and I figured why not, and next thing I knew I was driving to different locales every week to meet Hope's Realtor, a twenty-six-year-old whiz kid who made three times my salary and owned an RV park in East Tennessee. The whiz kid made me sign something that said I couldn't use another Realtor, and then on top of that said things like, "5:30 is kind of late. Could you meet me at 5 to go through the house?" And I would run out of work and drive eighty-five miles per hour down the freeway, getting there fifteen minutes late. Hope was always there and she would get more excited than the whiz kid as we walked through the homes. Hope would turn on lights, open closet doors, shake her head, nod, and ask what adjacent properties sold for.

There was one home in a historic suburb of Nashville that made Hope gasp as she walked through it, and she smiled and held her hands close to her chest like a woman in a silent movie. "Are you interested in it, Cameron? Because if you're not, I'm going to make an offer," Hope said. I assured her I couldn't afford it, but Hope could, and so she bought the house and kept her *Truman Show* house as well, renting it out.

The 1930s-era home had hardwood floors, brick fireplaces, and a finished attic. It looked like a place where you could shoot the Macy's Christmas catalog, and if you did, Hope could be the mom, and maybe I could be the young, hip dad, and in the photo we could watch our three-year-old son open a large box with a puppy inside, and Hope and I would toss our heads back and laugh.

Even though I just gave Hope a Polaroid of the chairs, we're not tossing our heads back, laughing. She smiled when I showed her the picture, said all the right things, they're perfect, I love them, but not twenty minutes later Hope is saying this is all too much — me, her . . . it's all too much. Hope is saying that she cares about me but that all we do is fight anymore and this isn't fun, and actually, it's just depressing. "I just have some issues with you that I can't move past," she says. "Trust issues." I'm not sure how it happened but she's now in a laundry basket, crying, her eyes so green, her lips so red. I feel a tear in the corner of my eye bulging like water through a plaster ceiling, but I hold it back.

And just like I did at the concert, I'm now seeing another time, another place. I see myself lying in bed, twelve years old, crying, telling my mom that I'm not good at anything. "What am I good at, Mom?" My mom puts her hand on my forehead and pushes my hair back and tells me all of the things I'm good at, none of which I now remember. "So many things," she said. "You're good at so many things."

I'm not sure why I think of this, but maybe it's because Hope looks like a little girl in that laundry basket and I want to tell her she's good and loved, just like my mom told me when I was so upset, but it appears she doesn't want to hear that. I tell her everything will be okay anyway, but I can tell she doesn't believe me from the way she wipes her eyes and looks down, avoiding me. As she does this, I notice Hope's bed, the thick white comforter, the Polaroid photo on top, and I realize it may be the last time I see the chairs.

It may be the last time I see Hope.

I should be more optimistic; we're just taking a break. I think that's how we left it, though I did say it might be permanent. Or did she say that?

Maybe I did.

I was trying to be strong.

I'm sitting on a bunk bed in what is now the guest room of my parents' house in Jackson, Michigan. My brother and I used to sleep on this bunk bed, he only six years old, and me, thirteen. At night we would listen to *Costas: Coast to Coast*, a sports radio show. My brother would ask me to keep it on, and though he didn't understand the topics, he liked asking me about the athletes Costas talked to, and I liked telling him about them.

I think of things like this when nothing else makes sense. Sports have always made sense. The Detroit teams are good, the other teams, bad. Easy. But this phone conversation that just ended, Hope crying just like she did last week in the laundry basket, wasn't so easy.

I've been in Michigan for the last few days, and each day, I've dreaded calling Hope. Our conversations have been full of how was your day, fine, how was yours, and each time, I'm thinking, *What else can I ask her?* Then I realize that I have nothing to say, and I feel sad and the conversation ends five minutes later, and when it does, my stomach hurts.

Ten minutes ago I spoke to her on the phone from this bedroom, and I said, "Well, maybe we should just break up, maybe that's what we need to do," and I waited for her to protest, but she didn't. "I feel like I'm being forced to do this," I said, "that you're waiting for me to say we should break up, and I guess we should."

Hope says she's sorry. She wishes things were different. "Maybe I'll feel different in a few weeks, I don't know, but I need some space."

I acted calm, but Hope's voice trembled and then broke in two. "Why do I always get like this in relationships? I don't want to feel this way," she said, crying. I thought of that song she gave me, the one with the word "disconnect," and I broke inside as I thought of it, though I didn't show Hope that I broke. "Well, the fact is, you *do* feel this way, so take some time, and maybe it will work out and maybe it won't," I said placidly. And then I told her that I loved her more than I ever loved my wife, and she said, "I love you too," and we hung up.

I loved you more than I ever loved my wife.

I actually said that, and I think it might even be true, not just one of those things you say when you're dying inside. Hope is the only girl I've ever wanted to marry. I didn't marry Sara because I wanted to; I married Sara because I didn't want to break up with her, which is a horrible thing to admit. But I *wanted* to marry Hope. I wanted to make that speech at our wedding, the one I never thought of giving Sara, the one where you say things you're supposed to say, like this is the best day of my life and Hope is my best friend, and if I could take anyone with me to a deserted island, it would be her. But in Hope's case, I would mean it. I wouldn't think to myself, *Act happy,* as she walked down the aisle, which is what I thought the day I married Sara.

I would instead think things like, *Don't get weepy,* because I would want to, the way I do when I watch that scene in *Glory* where Denzel and the other black Union soldiers are marching off to storm the Confederate fort, a sure death sentence, and the racist white Union soldier changes his tune and yells, "Give 'em hell, 54th!" The sacrifice is beautiful, just like it is in the best of marriages, the ones where people say to their spouse, "I give myself to you forsaking all other romantic relationships, and if I have to, I forsake my happiness for you, for better or worse, till death do us part."

There are stories I would've told at our wedding reception, things others never saw — how Hope and I walked down brick sidewalks on fall Saturdays, or how Hope tied my scarf, making this knot I could never make. I would tell people how the leaves fell on days like those and how we held coffee in white paper cups and saw our reflections in shop windows as steam came off the coffee. I would tell people how Hope said things like, "Why don't we go to Chicago next weekend and go Christmas shopping?"

I wanted to tell people how Hope encouraged me, always told me what a good writer I was, how she laughed at my jokes. I wanted to tell people how Hope looked into my eyes and always knew exactly what I was thinking, even when no one else did. I wanted to tell people how Hope liked Alfredo sauce on her breadsticks and how she bought things from infomercials sometimes, like Principal Secret face cream, and how she made me these whole wheat bagel sandwiches with salmon and capers and onions and cream cheese. I wanted to say I didn't care about the Donald Miller coffee meetings, and forgive me for being small and jealous sometimes, and I think it's great that you have a box of *Blue Like Jazz* and that you hand out copies to people because you think it might help them know God better.

I'm thinking of all these things, how the wedding speech will never happen, how those fall days are just a memory now, when suddenly my dad calls because he's home from work and wants to take me somewhere for lunch. He has no idea that I'm sitting on the bottom bunk in the guest room having just broken up with the girl I moved to Nashville for, the girl I thought would save me. I could sit here all afternoon, but instead I stand up and walk out the back door, trudging through the late December slush to my dad's car.

It's February, and I'm tired. I look out the window and it's 6 p.m. and black. I turn on my laptop and log on to the Internet. I'm sitting on the couch, thinking of Hope. Three weeks ago Sunday I called her. I knew I shouldn't have done that, but I've always had a negative association with Sundays and, well, it was Sunday and I was lonely. With Sara, Sundays were fluorescent grocery stores followed by questions like, "Why did you buy Doritos?" and "When are we going to use this mustard?" and "Didn't you realize we already had pasta?" Sundays felt like death.

But with Hope, Sundays meant dinner and three television shows that we liked. Sundays were a kiss at the end of the night, the beginning of another week with the woman I wanted to shout about. *This girl? Yes, she's with me*, I wanted to yell to anyone who would listen. The night I called, it was late January, Sunday, raining, and Hope didn't pick up the phone. I mentioned wanting to get coffee that evening—coffee as friends. "I have no agenda," I said in my phone message. "I just want to talk face-to-face as friends." Of course I had an agenda—I loved her, missed her, wanted her back—but "I have no agenda" seemed the right thing to say.

I called around 4 p.m., but at 5 p.m., no Hope. At 6 p.m., no Hope. *Maybe she'll call soon*, I thought. *There's still time to get together.* By 11 p.m. I knew she wasn't calling. She never called. I e-mailed almost a week later, and she e-mailed back, telling me that she didn't want to talk. I was too emotional. It wouldn't be healthy for her to meet with me. "When I break up with someone, I make it a clean break," she wrote.

I make it a clean break.

How did the girl who talked about marrying me only two months earlier never want to see me again? I once heard that life for most of us feels like a movie that we arrived to forty minutes late. I could identify. I knew the main characters in this movie, knew the ending, but there were pieces of it that just didn't make sense.

I think of all these things tonight, alone, the gurgle of the apartment refrigerator and the hum of my laptop the only sounds in my isolated world. I'm on the Internet tonight because I started an online journal just three days before Hope and I broke up. I'm trying to write about how hurt I am, how sad I've been, how everything reminds me of Hope, from *Grey's Anatomy*, the television show we once watched together, to the U2 song "Miracle Drug," which I told her to listen to when I realized that I loved her. She was my miracle drug; she took the pain away.

But as I write, I realize for the first time that I'm angry. The words coming out are not sad, as I imagined they would be, but bitter. *I moved down here for you and you just threw me away like trash. You used me until you no longer needed me. You're so selfish that I imagine that one day you'll just disappear, evaporate, because you have no need for anyone else, and no one else has any need for you.*

I get even angrier thinking of all the ways she hurt me. I think of how she laughed at me that night in the parking lot as I tried to find the restaurant. I think of how I helped her move furniture into the new house with her dad—gave up two days doing it—how that house was supposed to be ours one day, but now someone else will sit in those $1,200 chairs . . . maybe even the professional skateboarder who drives a BMW convertible.

As I'm thinking these things, I go to Hope's MySpace page, where I find photographs of her and the skateboarder, new photographs, photographs that look as if they were taken a week ago. I suspect she's dating him again, and yes, here it is, Hope calling him her "boyfriend." "My boyfriend, Tommy, had a big competition in Memphis this weekend. He's so great and I'm so happy we're back together." In the photograph, Hope is holding a glass of wine, smiling, her other arm around Tommy's neck. I look at the photo and feel fire in my veins. My face turns as red as Elmer Fudd's after Bugs Bunny hits him with a mallet. I think this rage will go away, that I can sleep it off, but I'm wrong. One week later I'm looking at Hope's MySpace page again, and the photo of Tommy is still there, and I'm on the phone with a friend saying things my friend can't believe I'm saying. "I've never heard you talk like this," he says. "You're really angry."

And then I say it.

"I hate her. I really hate her."

I have poison in my veins, venom, and I don't know how to get rid of it. I pray that God will take away the hatred, but it's still there. I try to let it go because the Bible says if we don't forgive those who have offended us, how can we expect God to forgive us? And it's a great question, one that I keep thinking of, which is why I tell myself, "Cam, you better get over it."

I just don't know how.

So one Friday night in late February, I e-mail Hope, telling her I'm angry, that I hate her. It's 11 p.m. when I send the e-mail, and at 11:45 p.m. her name lights up my phone. She's calling but I'm paralyzed, staring at the phone, not sure what to do. I let it go into voice mail, and sure enough, she leaves one. "That's really mature, not picking up the phone, Cameron. Whatever." And she's right. Two minutes later, she's calling again, but this time I pick it up. She says the same thing, and I say, "Is this really how you want to start our conversation, Hope?"

We bicker for a few minutes until I say, "Look, I e-mailed because I don't want to hate you, but I don't know what to do because I really do hate you. I just have this poison in me that I can't get rid of, and I want to talk to you about it."

Soon Hope is crying like a little girl. Not the way she cried in the laundry basket, but the way my sister cried when she fell off her bike and skinned her knee as a five-year-old. Through sobs, Hope says, "You don't know how hard this breakup has been on me, Cameron! It's not all about you . . . I hurt too, and I've never had chemistry with someone like I had it with you. I just didn't think we'd be able to make it work long-term." And then more sobbing, and she says, "And I'm so hurt by the things you've been writing about me on your blog . . . I know you don't use my name, but people know who it is and it really hurts."

Suddenly, all of my hatred melts away and I realize what a jerk I am, I realize that I just want to hold her, just like I wanted to the day she sat in the laundry basket, her eyes so green, her lips so red. I tear up and tell her I'm so sorry, so sorry, I care about you, I was just hurt, and don't you understand how much I love you, and can you even begin to imagine how it felt to lose the person you moved to another city for?

We talk for another hour, and it hurts because I know we won't get back together. "I miss you, Hope," and she sniffles and says, "I miss you too." I'm now standing outside, the sky clear, the conversation over, and I'm thinking about hatred — how I've felt it before but it's never disappeared like it did tonight. *It's easier to forgive someone when they show you how wounded they are.* Usually, in the heat of an argument, people exude an "I'm right, you're wrong" attitude, and I never get to see how wounded they are, how weak. But tonight, as Hope sobbed, I saw how pointless it was to hate. Looking at stars now, I see one flash across the sky and I'm reminded of the vastness of the universe. I'm also reminded of my smallness — my small attitudes, the small ways I hurt people.

If there is a time to hate, perhaps it's because there are some things I should hate: discrimination, pride, lies. Maybe the bottom line is that we all hate injustice, whatever form it takes, particularly forms that affect us. But I'm not sure we should ever hate people. We might hate what they've done, but we shouldn't hate them, and yet I hated Hope, hated her until I heard her cry.

But in that moment, I realized this wasn't a black-and-white situation. She wasn't all that bad; I wasn't all that good.

I don't hate Hope anymore; I'm just angry at life, unwilling to trust that God is permitting all this for a reason, that God knows what he's doing. I'm not trusting in anything other than my own vision, the here and now, what I can see. And all I see tonight is that I'm wounded and hurt and emotional and in disbelief about how this year is turning out. "Cameron, I think it's going to be a great year," Hope said that night in Denver, my birthday.

And I believed her.

I really believed her.

CHAPTER 5

A TIME TO LAUGH

So I commend the enjoyment of life, because there is nothing better for people under the sun than to eat and drink and be glad.[1]

It's New Year's Eve and I'm driving to P.F. Chang's to meet six people I hardly know, some of whom I met for the first time at a Bible study last week. The Bible study was held at the home of an attractive dark-haired woman, and as I pulled up to the attractive woman's home two weeks ago, I saw two Volvos parked in a circular driveway in front of a large picture window with warm lighting. There were tall trees in the front yard, and most of the neighboring homes could've passed for English manors. Clearly this was one of the older, more expensive parts of Nashville.

As I walked into the house, I was shocked. In the kitchen, on one counter, was a tray of cheeses, and on the other counter, three bottles of red wine next to a chilled bucket of specialty beers. That's right, I said specialty beers, not Miller Light or Natural Light or Pabst Blue Ribbon, but the sort of beer you buy at World Market with colorful labels and funky names and little animals on the labels. I knew I liked the Episcopalians, the denomination of the people in this Bible study, but this brought my admiration to a whole new level.

This was also perhaps just the thing to attract new converts, and it sent my mind racing. I started wondering why Christians had never tried it before. After all, didn't Benjamin Franklin say that beer was proof that God loved us and wanted us to be happy? Forget passing out tracts or yelling through megaphones. How about throwing a kegger at the Sigma Chi house? But then I remembered my friends from Wales, the ones who had started a pub church, and I realized it had all been done before.

My friends from Wales might be on to something though, because there was this liberating feeling I got while reading Scripture and drinking beer . . . really, more than liberating. I think it's fair to say that drinking beer while flipping through my Bible was a transcendental experience, at least for a kid who grew up in a Baptist church where you couldn't even have wine for Communion, only grape juice in thimble-sized plastic cups.

We rarely talk about that first miracle, the one where Jesus turns water into wine to keep the party going, but it's in the Bible. Mary asks her son to do something about the fact that they've run out of alcohol—a huge embarrassment for the wedding hosts—and Jesus tells her that his time has not yet come. But just as soon as you think that Jesus isn't going to do anything, you realize that when Mama's not happy, nobody's happy, because only a minute later, Jesus is creating some Merlot or Tawny Port or Petit Syrah, and the people at the party are amazed, saying things like, "Why did you wait so long to bring this stuff out? It's incredible."

I really enjoy red wine, though I'm not all that crazy about beer, something my Catholic and Episcopal friends would probably find heretical. And yet it was completely refreshing to drink beer that night and, in some small way, celebrate that first miracle of our Lord. It did a lot to change my image of Jesus as a finger-wagging naysayer, always throwing a wet blanket on fun, always looking to make you feel guilty, and what better way to dispel that myth than by mixing alcohol with Scripture?

And then I started thinking about other assumptions I make about Scripture, assumptions that may or may not be true. Of course, I've questioned so many things about God in the aftermath of my divorce and, as a result, stopped being so legalistic and scared of everything. I'm now open to the fact that I'm probably wrong about things, and other people probably are too. And yet my old way of thinking sometimes gets the best of me, because I occasionally worry that I'm not really a Christian at all, that maybe I have too many doubts, that maybe I have more in common with unbelievers than with people who are into Jesus. And maybe I do.

So if I do, why be around a bunch of Christians at a Bible study? I suppose to understand God better. I could probably trace this fascination with God back to my childhood: the felt boards with felt Bible characters stuck to them, the memory verses at my Lutheran grade school, the Bible camp at my Baptist church, where my friends and I walked our six-year-old selves into a room behind the sanctuary and prayed the "sinner's prayer" with our broad-shouldered pastor, the man who seemed a giant.

This was programming I just couldn't shake.

Or maybe it was more than that. Maybe there was this deep human need within me to know that there was a reason behind it all, to know that there was more to life than women and money and drinks and book deals. Or maybe I was simply worn down by the in-church commercials for the "young adults" Bible study, which I knew was church code for "attractive women."

After arriving back in Nashville last week, reeling from my breakup with Hope, it became clear that I knew virtually no one, no one unaffiliated with Hope at least, but I needed friends if I was ever going to get off my couch again. And what better friend to have than the woman who hosted the young adults Bible study, a woman who just so happened to be attractive and dark-haired? I knew this because someone had pointed her out to me at church one day, and from then on, I would watch her walk to the front of the sanctuary to receive Communion, and when she walked, I would notice her long legs and good posture and, well, what can I say? She made a strong impression on me.

That's why I'm at P.F. Chang's tonight. As I walk in, I see the dark-haired woman, probably early thirties, along with five other women at a table. So this is it, my post-Hope lifestyle — six women at a table and me — and, well, I can't really complain, can I? I can't, and yet I'm so sad that lifting a glass of water to my mouth feels like lifting a barbell, so sad that despite these attractive women I have all to myself, even the dark-haired woman who's smiling at me from across the table, I can't stop thinking about Hope. I wonder whom she'll be kissing at midnight as the calendar turns. For some reason, I picture her with a frosted-haired guy in an Abercrombie shirt, and that makes me sick to my stomach, but really picturing her with anyone tonight makes me sick to my stomach, frosted-haired or not.

I wonder if I can slink away quietly because I'm thinking of going home and vomiting, or maybe just lying in my bed in the fetal position as the clock strikes twelve. But I can't — not without making a scene I can't — because we're sitting in one of those enormous U-shaped restaurant booths and somehow after hugs and hellos and handshakes I ended up in the middle, three women squished in on each side of me, and if I tried to leave someone would undoubtedly ask, "Why in the world are you leaving so early?" and I wouldn't know what to say. Some people would think I'm crazy. "You're sitting with six women, let Hope go, there are plenty of fish in the sea, get back on that horse, cowboy," but it felt like a second divorce losing Hope, so it's really not quite that easy. I wish it were.

Fortunately, there's someone here who's easy to talk to, someone so calm that I can only compare her to a Zen rock garden. Her name is Sally, and she's sitting to my right, wearing a funky multicolored scarf straight out of a Dr. Seuss book. I remember Sally's name from Bible study last week because I had never met anyone named Sally that wasn't a poodle or a cartoon character. Sally has a certain ring to it, and the more I think of it, the more I like the name. There's something innocent and unpretentious about that name, something childlike, and I find that people who are childlike, not immature, but childlike, are typically the most sensitive and creative people on the planet.

Sally is one of those people—at least based on the brief conversation we had two weeks ago about how Larry Mullen gave her his drumstick at a U2 show. After she told me that story, I knew we were going to be friends. She also liked the U2 album *Achtung Baby*, and when I blanked on the name of a song from that album last week, Sally chimed in with the answer.

Sally has curly dark hair, hip brown-rimmed glasses, a British passport, and is, of all things, a youth pastor at the oldest Episcopal parish in Tennessee. As we begin talking, she tells me U2 stories, like how she knew this guy on the U2 road crew who got her seats to ten different shows on U2's *Elevation* tour. Ten shows? "Even one in England," she says quietly, hiding a smile.

Sally and I continue talking, but before I know it, it's time for Sally to go because she and her friend Cynthia, a young, attractive Episcopal priest, both have work tomorrow. "Unlike most people, we work on Sundays," Cynthia says. I smile and appreciate the irony, and I must feel reenergized, because as they leave, I agree to go with the other four girls to an eighties dance club, where we ring in the New Year as the DJ yells, "Celebrate!" and confetti falls from the ceiling. And as the confetti falls, the dark-haired woman tips her beer in my direction and smiles. I smile back and then look up, watching colored paper spin from the ceiling like tree leaves in a windstorm.

Sally was born in the middle of England but spent the bulk of her childhood in Cincinnati, Ohio, with two years in the Soviet Union sandwiched between life on that small island and life in the Buckeye state. I don't mean Sally lived in Russia for two years; I mean she lived in the Soviet Union, that place that existed before the Berlin Wall and Communism fell, back when there were all those jokes about the real Red Square being that strangely shaped mark on Gorbachev's head. That Soviet Union. But there was nothing really funny about the Soviet Union, not at the time, not with the arms race escalating and people's freedoms being trampled on. Sally remembers how foreigners couldn't go out after 9 p.m. She remembers living in a separate neighborhood for non-Russians, driving through the outskirts of Moscow, seeing cold, hungry people queuing in the streets for bread.

She's telling me these things two weeks after New Year's Eve. We're at Chili's eating salad and pasta, almost obscene portions in light of people queuing for bread, and I'm listening intently, fascinated with what she's saying about her British father being an engineer who worked for a multinational company. And even though Sally still has that red British passport, the U.S. is where she's lived since she was ten years old.

But despite some geographic stability—Sally's spent the last twenty-three years in the U.S.—her life is difficult for me to piece together, especially because she tells most of her stories out of chronological order, a tidbit here, a tidbit there, and it's a bit like trying to fit a puzzle together. Sally went to Northwestern University on scholarship, which for a Midwestern boy like me means something. Northwestern is the Harvard of the Big Ten, full of intellectuals who read literature in coffee shops, quite unlike the popular kids from my high school, the ones who went to Michigan State, double-majored in beer bongs and hallucinogens, and graduated in seven years. After Northwestern, Sally attended Ohio State for her master's in social work and eventually landed in youth ministry, which is what she's been doing ever since.

There's something deeper than deep in those tree-bark eyes of hers, and I can tell that our souls are talking to each other because out of the blue, I say, "You're in a lot of pain, aren't you?" And she says, "Yes." It takes one to know one, I think, and I find it strange that after the divorce, and now after Hope, I have this ability to spot people in deep pain, even those who project the happiest of façades. But Sally's much too wounded and honest to project a happy façade. Sure, maybe it's an "I'm okay" façade, but it's not a happy façade, because when she says, "Yes," to the wounded question, she follows it with, "But I'm okay," but that's said with a chiseled face and watery eyes and I can tell everything's not okay. And how could it be? Both of Sally's parents are dead, and as her father lay dying in a British hospital last month, her boyfriend broke up with her. And then right after the breakup, Dad finally died, and what do you do with that?

Sally didn't know what to do — all she had ever known was how to take care of other people. Her dad was a full-on alcoholic, her mom a functional one, and Sally remembers wrestling the keys from her mom's hand as Mom stumbled to the front door to take the car for a spin. She remembers how Dad lost his job, began drinking, and never worked again. He was homeless for six years, but Sally didn't let him stay homeless. No one knew where he was, but Sally found him and brought him back to England, and years later, he died there, back in his home country. Some of Sally's extended family was there when he died, but Sally had just spent a week with him in the hospital and couldn't stay any longer, and so her dad died while Sally was at a conference in the U.S.

The conference speaker was talking about spirituality, the lights dimmed, when at some point Sally and the other attendees were invited to place strips of paper in water. Sally's piece of paper said, "My parents," because people were supposed to write a burden they were carrying and then release it to God. Interestingly, the paper would dissolve when placed in water, symbolic of God taking those burdens away, and as Sally watched "My parents" dissolve into water, her dad, at that very moment, died in England.

He was cremated on Thanksgiving, his ashes sprinkled in the ground, and then a week later, Sally's only sibling became father to his first child. He named her Jane, which was Sally's mom's name. Sally was now an orphan, but a week after Dad died, Jane.

That sounds like something you make up, but as I sit here, listening to Sally talk over the dull roar of the Thursday bar crowd at Chili's, I know she's not making it up. Sally strikes me as a deeply spiritual person, and so it makes sense that something so deeply spiritual would happen to her. "The thing is," Sally says, holding back tears, "I finally have a family. My parents are finally whole. They're finally home."

This is someone I can learn from, I think to myself. *This is someone who understands life because she understands death.* My coworkers and I used to make fun of business guru Stephen Covey at my previous job because we all had to read his book *The Seven Habits of Highly Effective People*. But Covey is actually a brilliant guy, and one of the things he wrote stuck with me: "Begin with the end in mind."

Sally understands this, and perhaps, albeit quite late in life, so too did Solomon. And I'm starting to understand this too. I've never lost someone to death who I loved, but I have *lost someone*, most notably my wife, and then, of course, Hope. Life is fleeting, more so than I sometimes want to admit, and so it's often easier to just blow off discussions about death, to laugh about silly things, or to go and have a drink and talk nonsense. We're not doing that tonight, yet it's strange that in the midst of all of this serious talk, we begin joking again.

We're both so hurt, yet we're laughing.

We're not laughing because we're avoiding reality.

We're laughing because we've accepted it.

*

I'm starting to feel like myself again, which I attribute to the community of people around me. There's Sally, the mystical youth pastor and fellow U2 fan, and then there's Drew. I met Drew at a restaurant in October. Hope was out of town, and I was in a place called Jackson's with some coworkers. It was Friday after work and we were all eating chips and artichoke dip when Drew walked in and kissed his girlfriend, Ashley, on the cheek. I worked with Ashley but had never met Drew, but there he was at the end of the table, sandy blond hair, a fitted T-shirt, and a stocky, muscular build.

The first time I met Ashley was in the parking lot outside my glass office building. She told me she was divorced, and I said, "I'm so sorry," my face strained. But Ashley sharply said, "I'm not," and then laughed. Ashley has a South Carolina accent that sounds as sweet as honey or as tough as nails, depending on when you catch her. Looking at Drew, watching him lean toward the person across from him, his eyes wide, I could see how he had won over this spunky brunette.

I imagined Drew as one of the golden boys in high school, the guy who got all the girls, played all the pranks, made good grades, and went to college on a sports scholarship. Sure enough, I'm not that far off, because I learned that Drew played college soccer at Clemson. He has these huge blue eyes, which undoubtedly drives the ladies wild. He looks like he should be in a Land's End catalog, or maybe the next Gap commercial, and I sort of wished I looked like that.

But Drew never was a model; he was, of all things, a missionary to Russia. He went to seminary, learned Russian, and that night told me from his end of the table that he was working on a counseling degree. But what happened with the missionary stuff? Why did he leave Russia? He didn't really. One day his wife packed her things and left him and their two little girls in Russia. He followed her to Nashville because kids need their mom, Drew said, but she went off and had a baby with someone else and now she and Drew are divorced. I didn't get the opportunity to talk much to Drew that night, but later that evening I watched him hop in his black aging SUV, slam on the gas for twenty feet, and then screech to a halt. As the vehicle rocked backward, Drew jumped out, smiled, and yelled something at someone walking by, someone he must've known, before hopping back in the car and speeding away.

The second time I saw Drew, Hope and I were about to see *Walk the Line*, the Johnny Cash movie that Nashville native Reese Witherspoon won an Oscar for. We had some time before the movie started, so we drove down the street to a bookstore, which is where we saw Drew and Ashley roaming the aisles. We talked for a while, Hope talking to Ashley, me talking to Drew, and Drew said, "So you wrote a book? Well, we should write a book together sometime," and launched into his thoughts on theology and human behavior. I caught only every third word he said because I was trying to figure this guy out. He was unlike anyone I had ever known, certainly more intense than 99 percent of the people on the planet, and I thought that if I were ever able to call him my friend, I would be doing well for myself. Hope and I walked out and I said, "We should do something with them sometime. I think you'd like Ashley, and Drew is really cool." But we never did do something with Drew and Ashley.

In fact, the third time I saw Drew was after Hope and I broke up. It was early January and I was moping at my cubicle, preparing to eat saltines or something terribly depressing for lunch, when Ashley came around the corner and said, "Hey," and I swiveled in my chair and forced a smile and said, "Hey," back to her.

"What's wrong?" she said in that South Carolina accent, now sweet as honey. I sighed and said, "Well, I'm just sad, I guess . . . and confused about Hope." Ashley looked me straight in the eye, her face set, her small but muscular frame tense, and said, "We're going to lunch, and I'm calling Drew." I told Ashley I'd like that, and thirty minutes later, Ashley and I were at a sandwich place on the outskirts of downtown. It was a warm winter day, midfifties, and we sat outside eating pasta salad. Drew came late, barreling down the road in that black SUV of his, and we all sat and talked.

I felt like the center of attention, because both Drew and Ashley leaned forward and stared at me with no small amount of concern as I told them how sad I was and how I wondered what I had done to make Hope never want to see me again, and could this all be repaired? And Drew said, "First of all, you are whole and complete without her, and you must not think 'what if' right now, but only how you will respond in the moment."

Who talks like this? I wondered, but the more he talked, the better I felt. "You're confused, but that's okay. Confusion is clarity. You know you're confused. You don't have to know anything else right now." We talked for thirty more minutes like this, and I didn't want it to end, but Ashley and I had to go back to work, and Drew back to his windshield repair business, which he had started while deciding if he was going to go into counseling, or ministry, or something altogether different.

As Ashley smoked with the window cracked, I felt as if I had found my tribe, and I started thinking about how we were all just hurt little kids, all trying to find our way in the world. We all had our own dysfunctions and wounds and problems, but together those dysfunctions and wounds and problems looked almost beautiful, at least when we tried to help each other they did. When Ashley first met me, the day she said she wasn't sad about her divorce, she asked where I was from and I said, "Michigan," and she shook her head and in her antebellum drawl said, "Another damn Yankee." And I looked at her and smiled and had this feeling that underneath that tough exterior, there was this very soft, faithful person inside. I think of this now as I watch her smoke. She catches me looking at her and she looks back at me and smiles and says, "What are you grinning about?" And I keep smiling, look away, and say, "Nothing really."

Drew is very serious, but he also loves to laugh, despite the stress that comes with being a single dad, dating, and running a business. Tonight Drew and Ashley are having problems, so I tell him I'm coming over, coming over even though I live in an outlying suburb, coming over even though it's a Sunday night at 10 p.m. But I know Drew would be there for me on a Sunday night at 10 p.m., and so I want to be there for him. After a few wrong turns, I find his house. It's funny because I was never able to find his house when I first began hanging out with him — all those one-way streets and no big landmark to orient myself by — which would force me to sheepishly ask for directions. "Dude, I'm on Twelfth South. Where are you at again?" I would say from my cell phone, and Drew would laugh and tell me how to get there, just as he had done a week before, and probably the week before that.

I now have my route down, and I take it every time because I'd prefer to not have to call him for directions and look like an idiot. Drew lives just off Music Row in Nashville, and though it's not the best area, it's right next to Hillsboro Village, a hipster neighborhood where homes sell for $500,000. And I can't help but think Drew made a good investment, because all that Hillsboro hipness is bound to move his way; he's too close for it not to.

In lieu of not having a girlfriend to occupy my time, I've been spending lots of time with Drew, talking about life and relationships. It's February, just after 10 p.m., as I tap on the door and walk into his sparsely decorated one-story house. I see the kitchen table to my left, which holds a laptop, an open bottle of Newcastle, and a Bible. Drew comes from the back room to greet me and grabs his coat, but as we walk outside, we realize that it's probably a bit too cold to sit on the porch.

It's unfortunate, because the porch is our spot. It's where we typically sit at night with beer at our feet, talking about God or women, our hands stuffed in our coat pockets, our breath visible. And though we can see the Nashville skyline from his house, it's usually quiet, save the occasional car that rolls down the street, stops in the middle of the road, and waits for a man to come barreling out of an adjacent house and hand something to the driver, who then speeds away.

This usually happens around 11 p.m. and Drew and I make guesses as to what sorts of drugs are being purchased. "Eric from my church used to mentor that guy," Drew said one time, gesturing toward the nineteen-year-old wearing a dark parka, tailing it back into his house after handing the suspicious package to the driver. "He thought he had made a real turnaround. Maybe not."

Tonight, because of the cold, we don't sit out on that porch but deposit ourselves in his living room and talk of serious things, and then we're quiet. "You want a beer?" Drew asks, breaking the silence, and I say, "Sure." I don't really want one, but this is what Drew and I do; it's our way of bonding, and so he brings me a

Newcastle. I'm sitting on a couch on one side of the room, and he's sitting on a couch on the other side of the room, and as I take a sip, the beer somehow misses my lips. I'm really mystified as to how this could happen. I mean, I've been drinking liquids without a sippy top for the better part of twenty-seven years, and yet I just managed to spill beer all over Drew's couch. Drew looks at me with surprise and then just starts laughing. I play it off as a "drinking problem," and Drew grabs me another beer, wipes up the spilled beer with a kitchen towel, and I move over to the couch he's sitting on. As we joke about the spill, I take another sip and the beer again misses my lips and goes everywhere. I've never done anything like this, I feel like a moron, and now Drew is on the ground laughing. He's actually crying, he's laughing so hard.

Drew and I always laugh about these Jesus videos on the Internet. A church called Vintage 21 did a sermon series on what Jesus *really* said and did, and so the leaders of this church naturally made a series of videos on things Jesus *never* said and did—stereotypes that some people hold of God and Jesus and the church.

The Jesus videos are scenes from a kitschy Jesus film, circa 1960, with weird dubbed-over voices. So when you're watching Jesus overturn tables in the temple, the voice you hear is not an angry one but a placid, almost *Silence of the Lambs*–inspired voice saying, "There's that . . . there's that . . ." There's also a part where Jesus is talking to a crowd from a small hill—likely a reenactment of the biblical Sermon on the Mount—but the dubbed-over Jesus voice is saying things like, "You had your chance, but you blew it" and "There's no hope; you're all evil."

The people sitting in the crowd listening to this antimotivational speech look really pathetic, like Technicolor versions of ushers from my childhood Baptist church wearing fake beards, and Drew and I find it all quite funny. In another scene, Jesus says sharply to one of his disciples, "I hope you don't think you're going to the dance tonight, because you're not," implying that fun will not be tolerated.

Some people are offended by these videos, and if taken out of context, I can see why. But in the spirit of disabusing people of their notions of Jesus as someone who never had any fun, was always trying to catch people doing something wrong, and offered no real hope, these videos are brilliant. But I wonder if the general public really views *Christians* as the dour, self-righteous ones, not Jesus. I find when I ask someone who isn't a Christian about Jesus, their view is remarkably positive, but when I ask them about Christians, they become sullen and start using words like "self-righteous" and "annoying."

Drew is anything but annoying and self-righteous, and I think I could say that of all my new friends. Ironically, I wonder if sometimes losing ourselves to enjoyment and laughter isn't the holiest thing we can do. It seemed to be the thing to do the day Drew celebrated his thirty-third birthday. There were fifteen people gathered at his house, and as Ashley brought out the birthday cake, there was a picture of that kitschy 1960s Jesus on it, arms extended, and Drew laughed and extended his arms and did the strange voice.

And in my head, I thanked God for friends who could laugh, even in the midst of pain. I thanked God for Jesus, someone who could sympathize with us in our weaknesses. I thanked God for being a God who became human, a God who laughed.

*

It's almost spring, the end of February, and I'm standing in a restaurant called South Street in a neighborhood that doesn't seem like much of a neighborhood. There are some condos being built across the street, and I'm told that these condos will be the place to live once they're done. Not that I'll be able to afford them, but they'll be the place to live. South Street serves ribs and seafood, nothing great, but it's a good atmosphere, and the prices aren't too bad either. For dinner I've assembled a group of my favorite people—people like Sally, who is standing next to me now, or Drew and Ashley, who should be here soon.

As I fold my arms and lean against the wall, I look out the window and spot Rory walking toward the front door. His long legs seem to cross entire parking spaces with single strides. He's wearing a skullcap—a skin-tight version of a ski hat—and a navy blue peacoat. By night, Rory is a photographer, guitarist, and lead singer for a band called Copacabana, or Copa for short. Copa plays what Rory calls "Gospel Cigar Rock," and no one has any idea what that is, and I sort of think Rory likes it that way.

Sometimes when Rory performs, he lies on his back with his guitar, or he takes his microphone cord and uses it as a whip. And what does someone who uses a microphone cord as a whip do during the day? What else but work as a middle school detention supervisor. He's six feet, two inches tall, sandy brown hair, twenty-seven, and has a great face. It's not only a long and angular face but also one registered with a Nashville talent agency, and sometimes Rory gets calls for TV commercials or requests to appear in music videos.

Rory is from Minnesota, lived in Ohio for a time, and then moved to Tennessee, where he finished high school and went to college. He lived in Singapore for a year during college and while there appeared in a television commercial for a rice company. He tried to find that commercial recently on the Internet, but to no avail, and I'm sort of happy he didn't, because the rice commercial of my imagination is probably much funnier than the real thing. In my mind's eye, I see Rory smiling that wide smile of his and holding a fork to the sky while leaning over a steaming bowl of rice. There's a Far East pop song playing, and something weird is going on in the background, maybe people in red bear costumes, dancing.

Rory is now walking in with enough keys hanging from his belt loop to make a janitor envious. He sees me standing there with Sally waiting for a table and dramatically stops, slides his feet, and extends his hand toward me. I shake it and look into Rory's eyes, which are wide as frying pans. He shakes his head and looks mystified. "What's wrong? What happened?" I ask. I'm smiling because Rory's about to say something really interesting; I know it from the Cheshire cat smirk on his face. "We need to go next door after dinner. It's like L.A. over there. Or New York. It's Moroccan. A club. Wild." He makes a half circle with his head as he says "wild," his eyes pointing at the ceiling.

I met Rory at a barbecue last September. Hope was in Mississippi helping with hurricane cleanup, and I was at her business partner's house with eight couples. Eight couples and Rory. Rory and I were the only guys there without a significant other, and as I walked in, he said, "I like that coat you're wearing . . . very cool." It was a warm September night, candles everywhere, the sun almost down. We sat and talked, and when everyone else had left, Rory and I were still there at 11 p.m., and I thought, *This guy gets it.* He listens to the meanings underneath words. He notices things that most people don't.

But I did some noticing myself that night. I noticed that Rory's wife wasn't with him, but more than that, I noticed something was wrong. "Why isn't she here?" I asked. "She's tired," Rory said dismissively, and I looked at him and had a very bad feeling in my stomach. Two months later, Rory and I had breakfast and he told me that his wife left him, which is when I walked to my car and handed him my memoir on divorce, not knowing if it would really help, not knowing how it could help, but thinking it might provide some comfort.

"You're like the ghost of Christmas future, my big brother, me, one year in the future," Rory said at the time. "You're ahead of me in that you've been divorced and you can help me know what to expect."

Rory is talking to Sally when Caroline walks in. Caroline is the tall, thin brunette who I met at a work orientation–the girl I told Hope I was going to ask out.

The first few times Caroline and I talked, there was a weird electricity, and Caroline even suggested once that I come over to her house and she put her pajamas on and we watch movies together. "Seriously, it will be fun," she said. I thought that sounded like an interesting idea, especially after Hope, but it soon became clear that despite her long legs and model looks, Caroline and I were sort of like brother and sister. She worked in that tall glass office building with me, and I would take the elevator down to see her and lean on the walls of her cubicle until she turned around. And then one day she said, "You and I are going to be best friends, okay?" and I said, "Okay," and I tilted my head and smiled at her, and she said, "Yeah, best friends," and smiled back at me.

Caroline grew up in Florida, studied English at Auburn, and moved to Nashville after a stint with a humanitarian agency in Africa. Even though she grew up near Fort Myers, she's very Southern in her own way—her mostly Southern family has a history of duels and tractor accidents—and she's currently work-ing on a novel that begins in a muddy graveyard with a bunch of Southern women trying not to laugh during a funeral.

Caroline is excitable: she loves ideas, and she's most excited about whatever the latest idea is, whether that's a road trip to her dad's beach house or a public relations firm she wants to start. Caroline spent six months in Africa after college, and she still speaks of it as a magical place, the ancient dances, the moun-tains, the wildlife, the people who always manage to smile. When she starts talking about the time she spent working there, she slows her output of words, which usually fly like sparks from train wheels, and gets this far-off look in her eyes as if she's having an out-of-body experience. She really loves Africa.

Caroline has a nose that you can squeeze because there isn't much cartilage in it. It makes for an interesting party trick, and it's always funny to be somewhere with her and see people squeez-ing her nose. Caroline is also fiercely loyal, and when someone posted a nasty comment on my blog once, she pulled out a can of you-know-what and let them have it, anxiously calling me after-ward and saying, "Did you see what I wrote?" Caroline did that because she loves people deeply. She also loves cherry-flavored limeade, and sometimes during the workday around 3:30 p.m., she and I take the freight elevator downstairs and make a clandes-tine trip to Sonic. Sometimes I even carry a folder or a notebook to make it look like we're headed to a meeting. And though we say we're both going for a cherry-flavored limeade, I always get a Coney dog and Caroline laughs at me as she slurps her drink.

Sometimes I disappoint Caroline because she calls or text-messages or e-mails and I don't always call or text-message or e-mail back, but it's not because I don't care about her deeply—I do. I'm just ice to her fire, and my laid-back nature sometimes drives her frenetic personality a bit crazy. But here she is at South Street, now putting her arm around my neck, saying with intentional twang and a bit of shtick, "How are you, sugar?" As I give her a hug, Rory and Sally begin walking alongside our waitress to the table. Caroline, her boyfriend, Nathan, and I followed behind, and as we all sit down, Drew and Ashley appear. Ashley shuffles in on one end of the table, and next to her, Drew, follow by two other women who just arrived, and then me, Sally, Rory, Caroline, and Nathan.

"Cameron, we always said we'd never let women come between us, and now this," Drew says, pointing to the two female friends between us, and I laugh. As everyone begins to fool with their menus, I make introductions, "Everyone, this is Rory, and Drew, do you remember Sally? And Caroline, I think you met Sally a few weeks ago . . ." After we order our food, it's quiet for a moment, which is when Rory surveys the large table, leans in, and says to everyone, "I want to know something: Who's the happy clown at this table, and who's the sad clown? And who looks like the happy clown but deep down is really the sad clown?" Rory has an open look on his face, eager for an answer.

I'm eager for an answer too, but as I scan the faces of my friends, there are blank looks everywhere, people not knowing whether to laugh or raise their eyebrows or even attempt an answer. And I just smile, thinking, *Brilliant. What a brilliant question.* I say nothing but just watch the faces around me. And then I realize that maybe, just maybe, I'm the happy clown.

CHAPTER 6

A TIME TO GIVE UP

Yet when I surveyed all that my hands had done and what I had toiled to achieve, everything was meaningless, a chasing after the wind; nothing was gained under the sun.[1]

So I'm about to make a Bible video, which probably raises the question, "What is a Bible video?" Because there are so many Bible translations, publishers have a real challenge trying to convince the Bible-reading public that theirs is the best, so what you really need to do is convince the Christian bookstore that yours is the best, which is why most Bible publishers have what is commonly known as a "Bible training kit." Each Bible training kit includes information about Bible translation in general, but lots and lots of positive information about *that* company's Bible translation—words and phrases like "accurate," "readable," and "fits my lifestyle." The Christian bookstore employee is supposed to go through the kit and then decide that they like "X" Bible translation, and then when customers are trying to make sense of the 400 Bibles they're looking at, the employee can say, "Well, this is the one I like," and hopefully it's the Bible that your company makes.

So that's why I have a woman putting makeup on my face in a downtown building with high ceilings. I could act like a tough guy and tell you that I have no idea what she's doing, but let's be honest, I studied theater in college and took a theatrical makeup class, so I know exactly what she's doing. She's applying foundation, and then maybe she'll lighten the area under my eyes a bit, perhaps even give me a little something for my lips, but she hasn't gotten there yet, and I'm not going to remind her.

I always felt weird studying theater because I went to a conservative college and friends' mothers would look at me strangely when I told them I was spending a lot of time studying Einstein—not his theories, but how he walked and talked and the sort of person he was—because I was playing him in a show called, cheerily enough, *Insignificance*. One time, a friend's mom who homeschooled her kids in Iowa said, "Oh, so you're going to be an actor, are you? Are you going to go to Hollywood and live with all those immoral, self-absorbed people? My husband and I went to college with a guy who studied theater, and guess what he's doing now? Lawn care." I guess this friend's mom would feel better knowing I'm not currently employed in lawn care, but theater is what I'm doing today.

An advertising agency wrote a script for me to read on camera, which sounds something like this: "Hello, my name is Cameron Conant, and I'm here today to talk to you about XYZ Bible translation, which will help you connect customers with the Bible. This isn't a Bible training video. This is a Bible *experience*." The script then goes on to tell viewers that I, Cameron Conant, would like them to meet my "friends," people "just like me who have struggled to find time to read the Bible." The funny thing is, I've never met these friends, and, in fact, their photos were purchased from Photonica or some image warehouse. After the photos were purchased, the marketing firm attached fictional stories to the photos, and in a meeting two weeks ago someone said, "Why don't we have Cameron do the video? He's young and would look good on camera." And now here I am in a building with tall ceilings and my own makeup person and I'm supposed to read these stories.

I'm standing in front of a red couch with two cameras and tall yellow lights pointed at me, wearing a $175 pair of designer jeans that I bought at a boutique frequented by rock stars. ("You look hot, Cameron," said Hope, who suggested the rock star boutique in the first place.) Directly in front of me is a television screen with my script slowly scrolling down, and I start to sweat, my legs and voice shaking as I read.

"This is Darci. She's a friend of mine who lives in Philadelphia, a single mom, and she always struggled to read the Bible . . . that is until she found the XYZ Bible translation, which is written in everyday language. For the first time, Darci understands the Bible and is now attending a Bible study." Cut. "Cameron, okay, try that again. Your voice is a bit shaky."

We finish two hours later, and in those two hours I not only tell the camera about Darci but I also let the camera follow me through downtown streets as I buy ice cream and sit on park benches, looking at the sky. And as I look up, I notice thin clouds suspended below blue, which is when I think I was meant for something more than living out my days in a ten-story glass office building with Pepto-Bismol colored cubicles.

The company I work for is filled not only with pink cubicles but with forms and reports and meetings where people talk about things that never happen. I don't help matters any, and, in fact, I'm not a very good employee. I often just stare at the computer screen, a blank expression on my face. Sometimes I look at the flashing light on my phone, the one that indicates I have messages. I don't check my messages but instead think of something, anything, other than work. Sometimes I think about getting in my car and seeing how far I can get, maybe New York, where I'll board a steamship for Liverpool with only a journal, a pipe, and an old piece of luggage with stickers that say "Paris" and "London." On the boat, I'll meet the captain, maybe steer the ship, and spend lots of time drinking mojitos on deck, leaning against the railing in a navy blue pea coat, collar up, wind in my face.

In lieu of driving to New York and boarding that steamship, I go to lunch every day with a few coworkers. We go to the food court in a shopping center called Opry Mills, which is right next to the Grand Old Opry, a cavernous building where seventy-year-old country singers perform in rhinestone coats every Saturday night. Once in Opry Mills, I walk past the carousel, past the "You Can Be a Star" recording booth, to this place where they sell deli sandwiches, and I order a ham and cheese on wheat with tomatoes and banana peppers. My coworkers and I then eat and complain about work while mothers feed their babies creamed vegetables around us.

Sometimes after lunch we wander over to Barnes & Noble and order cappuccinos and I roam through the poetry and travel sections, fantasizing about sitting at a table for the rest of the day with a laptop, writing the great American novel, the one my high school English teacher told me I'd one day write. Strangely, part of me always believed her, and still does, even though the closest I've gotten to that great American novel is a Sunday business article for the *Grand Rapids Press,* in which I gave a creative account of my experience in a day spa. For the article a photographer took a photo of me, shirtless, getting a hot stone massage, and my female editor thought it was all very funny. I remember wondering how my wife was going to react, me disrobed on a table, a curvy, young Russian woman putting her hands, or, I guess, rocks on me, and I knew I had to be very careful how I wrote that article so as not to upset my wife. In the end, I think I made it sound like I really didn't like the massage all that much, but I really did.

Of course, I've written a book, which I suppose is closer to the great American novel than a business article on the day spa industry, but not much. Some people tell me my book is really good, and I think parts of it are decent, but parts of it make me cringe — a bad sentence here, poor word choice there, a typo here, a lousy paragraph there — and I always hope that I haven't written something I'll want to burn in ten years. But for now, I don't feel that way. In fact, I'll often walk through the religion section or relationship section or any section where they might have my book, and I'll look desperately for its spine, and when I see it, I'll position it face out, letting people know that it is not only available but also likes long walks on the beach, never has bad breath, and is very witty, though clearly a bit moody at times.

But this particular Barnes & Noble, the one near the food court at Opry Mills, never has my book, and I always feel a tinge of sadness when I don't see it on the shelf. And then right about the time I realize that, no, they don't have my book, it sinks in for the millionth time that it will never be a *New York Times* best seller or any kind of best seller. But before I completely lose myself in thought, I see my coworkers standing near the door, patiently waiting for me, ready to drive back to work. That ten-minute drive feels like ten seconds because my coworker Krista, plays a U2 album, or sometimes a Counting Crows CD, and before I know it I'm hitting the ceiling and she's tapping her thumbs on the steering wheel as we listen to "Omaha" or "The Fly." We don't want to go back to the office building because part of us dies when we walk in there, and who wants to stop listening to U2 or Counting Crows? We don't.

Before Hope and I broke up, I tried to make a career for myself in publishing, decided that I could be a "publisher" someday, mainly because it sounded cool, but also because I saw myself as more of the editorial sort than the marketing sort, and apparently publishers do things like decide what books to publish. I also thought I could make some real money as a publisher, which would allow me to buy a big house in the suburbs, go to fancy wine parties, and sound impressive when I told people what I did, not that I didn't sound impressive now, saying I was a "director," but sound even more impressive. But then I learned that publishers did lots of things with numbers and projection sheets and they had manila folders everywhere, and I knew I would be lousy with numbers and manila folders, so I quietly gave up the dream.

After six months at the company, I know I have to leave. My cubicle feels like a bunker, and I, a soldier, trying not to get shot. I feel surrounded on all sides — a vice president in the tree with a sniper, a human resources official over the next hill, about to throw a grenade. Behind me, people from accounting are on their bellies, inching closer to the overdue invoice on my chair. I think of this weird, military-inspired vision on a cloudy, wet Wednesday afternoon in March, six months after that Bible video, drinking coffee from a Styrofoam cup — black, three-quarters full. This job feels like war, but the bullets are not made of lead but of words, the assaults not from long-range missiles but from men and women wearing business slacks and nice shoes.

"I'd like you to get a good performance review, so let's go over your job description," I remember my boss saying one day, his door closed. "You don't do a very good job reporting, but your counterpart in the other department over there does. You need to get better at that if you ever want to beat her out for a promotion or get a good review from me."

I'll go for blood if I play you in Trivial Pursuit or tennis or basketball, but I wave the white flag when it comes to office politics. I don't see the winner of a political tug-of-war as better than the loser, usually just more manipulative. My dad is the same way. In the eighties my dad was playing Pictionary when, according to legend, his team couldn't guess what he was drawing, which is when he proceeded to throw his pencil in frustration — the only problem being that the pencil didn't hit the ground but lodged itself in a woman's hand. This story is still only whispered about because my dad frowns when it's mentioned, and he doesn't frown often. But like my dad — who, though a much-loved attorney, never had much interest in running for judge or prosecutor — politics don't interest me, and I too would be frustrated if you couldn't guess what I was drawing during a heated game of Pictionary. Come on, it's a dog, it's obvious . . . see the tail?

This job doesn't interest me. I dislike writing my account number on my monthly check to Tennessee Electric, so imagine how I feel filling out a work request for a ten-digit account number that I then have to write on another form which then has to be signed by my boss and someone else in marketing and then sent to someone in accounting who then sends it back to me, which is when I sign it myself. I think I then have to do a rain dance around it and solve a few algebraic equations, maybe write a short essay on why pi is 3.14, and all to get a production company $2,500 for making a promotional video.

Getting a check cut sometimes takes five phone calls, seven e-mails, and three weeks, and by that time, I've forgotten who needs a check in the first place, which is a problem because I'm sometimes asked in e-mails, "Who is this check for?" Now, I might have a manila folder telling me whom the check is for, but I can't tell you where that folder is because I'm not good with manila folders. I'm always reminded of this when I peer over my Pepto-Bismol–colored wall, which is Ted's cubicle, and see manila folders in neat rows, alphabetized by topic, all in Ted's careful handwriting, which should be its own font.

A few months ago, I wanted to bring a speaker to the ten-story glass office building, a speaker who said really interesting things about marketing, and so my boss said to put a proposal together, and I put a proposal together, and then my boss said he couldn't approve my proposal, that I should send it to his boss, and so I sent it to his boss, and then someone told me that his boss couldn't do anything with it, that it probably had to go to the CEO, or maybe the CFO, and I never heard about it again.

I was disappointed, but not deterred from aiming high, because weeks later I had this really interesting idea for a new type of book. I ambled down the hallway to tell one of the important people my new book idea, and he looked at me like I had twelve heads and quickly switched the topic, asking why I never turned in this one form, but when he said it, I knew there were so many I hadn't turned in that I couldn't imagine which one he was talking about. I felt my interest in the job going down like the *Titanic*. I couldn't wait to go back to my desk and daydream about that steamship to Liverpool or maybe a boat ride along the coast of Croatia.

I was made for this job like toothpaste is made for jet engines. I think of how one of the important people gave me a box of videotapes once, footage of her on news shows talking to well-known reporters about publishing or religion, and I said thanks and then, for some reason, threw them away. To her horror, I disposed of her only evidence that she had ever talked to Lou Dobbs and Matt Lauer and who knows who else. I threw the tapes away in my gray rectangular wastebasket because I didn't need them, and, well, I thought she would have backup tapes. And if she didn't, why in the world would she entrust them to me, someone who was bad with manila folders? She must've known I was bad with manila folders — one look at my desk would've told her so. Unfortunately, she didn't have other tapes, which explains why she cringed every time she saw me and then turned her cringe into the saddest excuse for a smile you've ever seen, sort of the way I smiled as a twelve-year-old when my grandmother gave me a New Kids on the Block videotape for Christmas.

I take another sip of my coffee on this rainy March day and remember the many meetings I've had with my boss, Michael, the silver-haired man. I remember epic battles fought, sneak attacks launched, bluffs made, counter-offensives waged, and unexpected retreats. Three months earlier, I sat in his office as he pulled out a folder. He said there were missed deadlines in that folder, and then he pushed the documents across his aircraft carrier–sized desk. I didn't look. "I have e-mails showing how you didn't follow through with assignments. And it looks like I haven't received notes from your one-on-ones in a couple of months. I've asked you to take notes and send them to me after every one of our meetings, and you haven't."

Of course he was right, but didn't he understand that I had things to do? Important things . . . like watching my phone flash and daydreaming about steamships, and, well, who ever heard of taking notes during one-on-one meetings, and why can't we just call them "meetings" instead of "one-on-ones"? And while we're at it, why do companies abbreviate everything, because as much as I don't like the phrase "one-on-one," it's much better than "OOO," which my boss's assistant always writes on my office calendar.

"You know, it's going to be difficult for you to rebuild trust with me. It's possible, but it's going to be a long road for you, and it's going to take a lot of effort on your part, and you might not be up to it." I sat there dumbfounded. "Are you trying to force me out?" I asked. "I don't understand why you're doing this, why you have a file on me. If you have a problem with something I've done, let's talk about it. I'm really blown away right now." Michael sat there and moved his mouth, his silver hair bouncing up and down. His jaw moved, words came out, but I heard no sound. I tried to focus on a particular part of his face, just as a driver tries to focus on the solid white line that runs alongside the edge of the road to keep him from flying into a tree. My focal point was his mouth. I saw his lips contorting themselves in various positions, seemingly in slow motion.

This wasn't the first time I had been surprised at work. Shortly after I started, I was asked to present a marketing plan to a group of executives and sales people, a plan that months earlier Michael and a team of outside firms had created. I had little to nothing to do with that plan but felt honored to present it, mainly because only eight people in the company were asked to present plans, me being one of them, and, well, that must mean something. Maybe important people will be at my presentation and they'll point and say, "That Cameron is really something; he has a future here. Look at him up there, the way he points and gestures and makes witty jokes without really even trying. I think that young man is executive material. I even heard he threw away those old videotapes of Kristin's, the ones of her talking to Matt Lauer and Lou Dobbs. Brilliant. Think of what he was saying: 'I'm not interested in the past . . . I'm interested in the future.' This kid's brilliant."

If I played my cards right, maybe *I* could be an important person whispering things about talented young employees while sitting in the back of conference rooms; maybe I could go to executive-only Christmas parties and chicken lunches with balding men in overpriced convertibles. *But see, these things will never happen*, I think to myself a week before I'm to make the presentation. *The right people will never talk about how good I am — not if I present this plan, they won't.* After all, one of the big ideas involved having a former reality show contestant say how much he liked the Bible, and I guess people were supposed to not only be excited about that but then go and buy one of our Bibles at their local Christian bookstore. I worried that people would think these were my ideas, not someone else's. Perception was everything.

What was I doing? What was I saying? I wasn't political, but here I was, plotting how to get ahead, how to make myself bigger, better, wealthier, and all by "effectively marketing" the Bible, all by trying to impress the "right" people. What was wrong with me? How weird was this, me maneuvering, posturing, and all in the name of marketing a book that I hardly lived by. I was reminded of how a long-haired evangelist put a half-eaten apple on the podium at summer camp to demonstrate how "life rots" — his point being that we needed to live for something that wouldn't decay. But something tells me that if I've done anything at all in this job, it *will* rot, if it hasn't already. The shuffled papers, the phone calls, the work requests, the promotional videos, the running, the sitting, the chasing, the being chased, it's all just spitting into the wind, just smoke. "So what do you get from a life of hard labor? Pain and grief from dawn to dusk," Solomon wrote. "Never a decent night's rest. Nothing but smoke."[2]

A magazine advertisement for the Bible. Smoke. Fictional stories read on camera by a twenty-eight-year-old wearing a ridiculous pair of $175 blue jeans. Smoke. A book on divorce that Barnes & Noble doesn't carry. Smoke. A good salary. Smoke. Forms. Smoke. Reports. Smoke. A silly presentation for sales executives. Smoke. The girl you worked so hard to get. Smoke.

I didn't think any of this the day I took the elevator to the seventh floor. I wanted to be a trouper and keep my mouth shut, but instead I found myself in the office of a short forty-something executive. Bill had sandy blond hair, gray on the sides, and was one of the top executives in the company. Stepping into his office, I was surrounded by photos of birds, several of which looked like hawks, or maybe eagles. Whatever they were, they had talons, and I thought of Napoleon Dynamite asking, "Do chickens have talons?" just before he tepidly cleaned hundreds of chicken coops.

"Well, I came by to talk to you about something," I began. "I basically wanted to let you know that the marketing plan that I'm presenting on Thursday . . . well, I didn't create it. I'm honored to present it, but I guess I just wanted you to know that the ideas I'm presenting aren't mine." *That was good, Cam. That's how these business types like things: real short and sweet and matter-of-fact. No bull; just the facts. Nice job.* But Bill's face turned ashen and he said nothing. *Wait, okay, maybe he didn't like that. Maybe it was too direct. Soften your statement a little; give him some context.* "I, uh, I think there are a lot of good ideas in the plan; I just probably would've done it a bit differently, and I guess I just wanted you to know that it isn't my plan," I said.

Silence.

"Cameron," Bill said as he put his hands behind his head and leaned back in his chair, "have you ever read a book called *Good to Great*?" A lump formed in my throat. "No, but I'm familiar with it. It's written by Jim Collins, I believe." *Where's he going with this? This doesn't sound good. At least I knew the book was written by Jim Collins . . . maybe that counts for something.*

"Jim Collins, yes, I think that's right," Bill said dismissively. "Well, in the book it says that in business, you go into a meeting and battle it out, but if your idea loses, well, you still come out of that meeting with arms locked." He moved his arms to show what "arms locked" looked like. "I just don't understand why you're in here telling me this," Bill said, his voice reflecting a hint of irritation.

The lump in my throat returned.

"Well, you know, just, um, like I said, I wanted you to know that I'm happy to present this plan, and it has a lot of good ideas in it, but that I didn't create it."

Silence.

"So basically you're telling me you didn't create this crappy plan," Bill finally said, this time with a wink and a mischievous smile.

"No, I'm not saying that it's crappy, but, yes, I'm saying that I didn't create it."

"Well, all right," he said.

I walked out of the office feeling as if I had just put a noose around my neck. I feared being branded as the one who created this largely unimaginative plan, which is why I had approached Bill that day, but it quickly became obvious that my visit was less than successful. I thought of that picture in his office of the hawk with large talons . . . or was it an eagle?

I began doubting myself. I wasn't a detail person—that became abundantly clear early on. My desk looked as if it had vomited paper; my idea of meeting notes included large cartoon-like sketches; I was often fifteen minutes late; and it was a small miracle if I handed in my weekly report early. I didn't like bureau-cracy, and when something didn't make sense, I insisted we do it another way.

It was a climate almost opposite to the one I had known in my previous job, and I soon realized that I was indeed a bad fit for the company, a bad fit for the position—but hadn't I been honest about my shortcomings in the interview process? I thought I had made it clear that I didn't like bureaucracy ("Oh, I agree, I don't either," Michael, the silver-haired man, had said) and that I was a "big-picture person."

Michael was my complete opposite. He arrived early, meticu-lously reported his progress to those above him, and kept close tabs on the most mundane details—something I had difficulty doing. Still standing in my cubicle, still lost in reverie, I take another sip of black coffee, remembering my first meeting with Michael.

We were at Starbucks in Nashville ten months earlier to discuss the job, two months before our clandestine Denver lunch. I was in town to see Hope, but we scheduled the meeting to coincide with my visit, Hope dropping me off at the front door and then slinking away because she knew Michael and he knew her but he didn't know we were dating, or seeing each other, or whatever it was then. "I see myself as a life coach," Michael said twenty minutes after Hope left. It was a ninety-degree day and

Michael was sipping mocha, sitting in a chair on the outdoor patio. His young daughter sat next to him and said nothing, her face buried in a comic book. "If you come and work for me, I want to help you get where you want to go — whether that's somewhere else in the company, or into a different career altogether."

I wanted to believe him, but I never felt completely comfortable taking the job — I couldn't figure Michael out and whether he was being straight with me — but I accepted it anyway. I accepted for Hope: hope that life would be better than it was in Michigan. Hope that more money and an impressive-sounding title would make me feel like someone. Hope that Hope would always be there.

Little did I know that I would one day stare at the white conference room wall during a meeting with Michael, alone, no Hope, imagining myself in another place, another time . . . at the top of the Eiffel Tower; watching a bullfight in Valencia, Spain; at a Detroit Tigers spring training game in Lakeland, Florida. Anywhere other than that dead, whitewashed room, beige carpet, a faceless corporate building, nowhere, USA.

And now I was supposed to report on what I was doing more often — me, the guy who couldn't even organize manila folders or fill out forms correctly. I already spent much of my time reporting, from the report where I listed my accomplishments for that week (example: "brainstormed creative ways to engage the customer"; translation: "stared at my computer screen and thought about drinking mojitos on a steamship bound for England"), to the daily report where I listed what I was working on that day, to the reports I gave during my weekly one-on-one (OOO) meetings.

And now they needed more reports.

And I decided that what I needed to do was leave.

CHAPTER 7

A TIME TO REFRAIN

There is a time for everything, and a season for every activity under the heavens: . . . a time to embrace and a time to refrain.[1]

It's Monday morning and I have dark circles around my eyes. I feel as if I have mono, but, no, I'm just tired . . . and sad. I'm sitting at my Pepto-Bismol cubicle, checking e-mail, ignoring the scores of e-mails with red exclamation points next to them. Suddenly I see one that interests me. "Subject: Thank you for your insight." Each week I get a handful of encouraging e-mails from people who've read my book, so I eagerly click on this one, hoping it will provide the boost I need to get me through a day of meetings and phone calls, and reports where I document those meetings and phone calls. It says:

> Cameron,
> It's probably strange that I'm writing you, because I don't know you, but I read an article you wrote in a magazine

and I wanted to say that it really connected with me. I debated writing you for a long time, not wanting you to think I was some crazy fan, but I finally decided that you might like to hear that you had a very strong impact on me and that I appreciated very much what you had to say. You are a wonderful writer. I live in Nashville and know Michelle Stark, who I think you know. I am also interested in journalism, and I know you were once a newspaper reporter. Any advice?
Erica

I smile and move on to something more pressing, but the e-mail stays with me, especially because Erica knows someone I know and her message is sweet and flattering. And I go to bed realizing that Erica's e-mail was the only bright spot in my day, which is why I'm opening it again today, writing this response:

Erica,
It's great to hear from you. Thank you for your kind words. So you're interested in journalism? Do you have any experience? Did you study journalism in college? The best way to get started is to either intern somewhere or freelance for a newspaper so you can accumulate "clips." Like anything, you need experience in order to get a job, but no one wants to hire someone without experience, so freelancing and interning are your best bets. I'd be happy to have coffee with you sometime and talk about this further if you'd like.
Cameron

I surprise myself by writing, "I'd be happy to have coffee

with you sometime" because, though it's been two months since I broke up with Hope, I'm no closer to being over her than I am to winning the Mr. Universe title, which at 157 pounds isn't happening anytime soon. I still can't get myself to read *If You Want to Write*, the book Hope sent me when I lived in Michigan, the one in which she wrote, "From an aspiring writer to an accomplished one!" I knew that wasn't true, me being accomplished, but I blushed when I read it and then put it down and read it again two minutes later. It's currently buried underneath four other books on my nightstand, and sometimes I notice its spine and feel as if I might throw up or cry or just sit on the floor with my eyes closed. I can't even listen to the songs we once liked, not the rendition of "Fields of Gold" by Eva Cassidy, not the David Mead song "Nashville," nor can I drive near Hope's house because I just see our ghosts walking down those brick sidewalks, peering into shop windows.

Most mornings I don't want to get out of bed. I see each day as a series of small steps because to think of an entire day is too overwhelming for me. Step one: Turn off the alarm. Step two: Stand up and walk to the shower. My days are composed of very simple tasks, and starting a new relationship is far from simple. A girlfriend is the last thing on my mind as I walk into Starbucks to meet Erica. It's a cold winter night as I open the door, and I just want to go to bed, just want to tell her, "I'm sorry, but I'm just not feeling very well and I shouldn't have offered to have coffee with you."

But I'd be lying if I said I didn't at least do some investigative work before walking through these doors, because I googled Erica's name and found a photo of her. She was pretty, but I observed she was pretty like I observed that it was sunny yesterday. I hoped for a little conversation about journalism, really nothing more, but I couldn't help looking for her photo because I have this habit of admiring the way beautiful women look and I wondered if she was beautiful. And she was. But I told myself then, and tonight, that none of that matters, that only helping someone matters, and helping Erica might be just the thing to get me out of my funk. And maybe it is, because as I walk to the counter to order coffee, I notice a tall blonde woman alone at a table, and my resolve to leave disappears. I look away, and she looks back, and I look back, and we both say, "Are you . . .?" and we smile. The way she smiles tells me it's okay, that I don't need to leave, that it won't hurt to talk to her, that it might even do me some good.

Two hours later, my coffee is gone and I'm leaning across the table, my eyes fixed on hers. Erica is describing the car accident that killed her fiancé, how his car rolled across the empty freeway and into a ditch. Erica was a quarter of a mile behind in her car as she watched his body fly through the night air like a crash test dummy. When it did, she stopped her car and screamed, just screamed into the icy, deserted air, and no one heard her, no one came to help. Erica stumbled out of her car and found him on the side of the road and touched him, blood everywhere, and someone finally stopped their car in the middle of the highway and yelled, "Are you okay?" and Erica just screamed.

My eyes are clear and glassy, and Erica's are clear and glassy, as she finishes the story . . . the ambulance, the hospital, more screaming, tubes in arms, people in the hallway, prayers cutting through that icy, deserted air. Erica leaves no detail untouched. After the story, we walk to the parking lot and exchange cell phone numbers, say we should meet again, and Erica hugs me. I'm a physical person, but Erica hugs me the way I'd hug my sister after not seeing her for six months, not the way I'd hug a complete stranger. Erica feels as if she knows me. She read my book—told me that an hour ago—and also reads my blog. I hug her back, my body still hurting, still sad, and I think, *Next step: Walk to the car.*

And I walk to my car.

*

A few days later, I call Erica and ask if she might like to do something, and she says, "No, I'm sorry, I have plans," and I think, *Of course you do. You seem a compassionate and interesting person and, well, beautiful, so of course you have plans.* I just wanted a friend for the evening, and the way Erica hugged me, the way she told me her story, I thought we might be friends. And we might be.

But I didn't need to hear she had plans—not tonight, because tonight I'm empty, and as much as I want to pray about the emptiness, I turn on my laptop and begin looking at pornography. I haven't done this in six months, maybe more, but here I am looking at images of naked women, stuff that would make most people blush. But no one's calling, no one's around, no one cares, and so why not go for a little gratification?

I'm alone on my couch, trying to cross the Grand Canyon in my heart on a bridge of toothpicks. I say toothpicks because these pictures of naked women are flimsy material, but I keep looking anyway because it gets me high like a drug, just like Hope did. Strangely, I only reach for porn when I'm running from something. I'd rather look at naked women than have that difficult conversation or make the hard decision or work through the pain. But the porn high quickly wears off, and when it does, I feel terrible and dirty and weak. I then go six, seven, eight months without looking at it — it's not even a temptation, and then my world blows up and I fall into the canyon, wondering how I got there, wondering how to get out.

Most women I know don't understand pornography. I remember how my ex-wife's eyes narrowed and her mouth tightened when she first learned I looked at pornography. I remember how she yelled at me and said I was dirty and went into our bedroom and locked the door behind her. I stood outside for ten minutes, my hand on the doorknob, saying in a hushed voice, "Sara, let me in," and she said nothing. Other women I know aren't all that different; they too think pornography is very sick and dirty and perverted, and they're right, yet I recognize what a temptation it is for decent men, what a temptation it is for me. But I didn't always think this way.

I remember being a twelve-year-old kid, years before the Internet made pornography as accessible as cable TV, listening to a rancher in tight Wrangler jeans talk to my church youth group about his struggles with pornography. Somehow I got the impression that only strange, socially awkward guys in tight Wrangler jeans with bad childhoods struggled with porn, but I don't think that's true. In the Scriptures, there's this story about how King David, Solomon's father, was on the roof of his palace once when he saw a woman bathing. I imagine she was stunningly beautiful, and David must've thought so too, because he didn't look away but watched her. David had things on his mind, most notably a war he was fighting, and so a naked woman was probably a welcome diversion.

And so, too, for me, pornography is a welcome diversion, which, strangely, makes me think of that part in Scripture where Jesus talks about how he is the vine and we are the branches, and if we remain in him, we will bear much fruit. And I wonder,

Where's the fruit in my life? All I see is an ugly history of websites that needs to be deleted from my computer, which I do just before falling into bed and picking up a book from my nightstand, the one Hope gave me about writing. And for some reason, maybe to punish myself, I read what she wrote on that first page.

"From an aspiring writer to an accomplished one!"

I know that isn't true, me being accomplished.

But then again, none of it is.

And I put the book down, turn off the light, and close my eyes.

I did hear from Erica again. She called two weeks after coffee to tell me she was at a book conference in Nashville visiting a friend of hers, and knowing I was in publishing, she wondered if I was there too. I was there, but I got her message just as I was leaving to have drinks with some old work friends from Michigan. I didn't have much time to talk, so I didn't call her back. But after onion rings and chicken wings and lots of laughs and a Jack Daniels straight, or "neat," as my friend from Michigan says, I open my car door, thinking I should've called Erica back. But it's much too late now.

So here I am, in my dark car, devastated, hurt, upset, and I can hardly put my finger on what it is. I suppose it's the death of a dream, namely, Hope, and maybe the lesson is not to pin all your dreams on one person. I'm thinking this as I put in a Coldplay CD and play the song "Fix You," the one in which Chris Martin sings, "When you try your best, but you don't succeed/ When you get what you want but not what you need." As I play that song, I fly out of the parking lot and hit the highway at 80 miles per hour. I watch my speedometer climb, 85, 90, 95 . . . I'm blowing past construction barrels, and as the road becomes an empty three-lane highway, I hit 100, 101, 102, 103, 104, 105. It's 1:24 a.m. and I'm daring the police to stop me. I don't really care if they do. I don't really care if I crash, either, which at 105 would leave me in pretty bad shape.

I get home with no police lights, no accidents, and fall into bed, thinking I should probably call Erica tomorrow. But tonight Hope is the one I want to call. And why not? No one's here to tell me we're bad for each other or that it isn't the right time or that marrying Hope isn't in God's plan. I'm thinking of Hope four weeks later as Erica and I stand on the roof of a parking garage. Rory said it's a great place to see the Nashville skyline, and he's right. Erica's standing next to me and we're leaning over the railing, the icy wind blowing. I look to my right and see Erica's long blonde hair twisting in the wind, and she looks at me, smiling. I smile back, but it's more of a grimace because there's pain there—deep, aching pain. As wonderful as Erica is, as pretty as she is, she's not Hope.

Erica and I went out four or five times before we ever kissed because I worried about how I'd feel, how she'd feel, if we did. And then one night we were sitting on my dark green couch tickling each other, my face close enough to see the smallest freckle on her nose, when the laughter stopped. It was at that point that Erica got a very serious look on her face, the corners of her mouth upside down, and I kissed her. I expected a small kiss back, but instead she swallowed my face, her lips like red plungers. I laughed and Erica asked what I was laughing about. I said I was laughing because I was happy, and she said, "Oh." When Erica left that night, I felt good, tall, proud—proud just like the skyscrapers I see from the top of this concrete structure. I notice how the buildings flicker like tea lights, and I see their reflection in Erica's eyes. Most writers would say this is the perfect scene for lovers in love, but I'm not sure if I'm in love, or should be, or could be.

And yet here we are talking about relationships, and I'm saying, "I don't think people get married because they want to be loved. I think it's something much more basic than that." Erica looks at me quizzically, her face framed by skyscrapers and dark clouds and a partial moon. "I think we all want someone to witness that we mattered, that we hurt, that we laughed, that we lived. That's why I write: I want people to witness that I lived." It's quiet but for the low howl of wind, and after a minute or two, Erica wraps her arms around me, pressing her cold cheek against mine. I touch her hair and kiss her forehead and look at those small Nashville streets.

And I wonder where Hope is.

Erica is about my height, except when she wears heels, which is when she becomes six feet tall, and I, sadly, remain five foot ten inches. But her height doesn't bother me. She's the definition of a blonde bombshell: hair that goes down her back forever, long legs, broad shoulders, perfect skin, and a symmetrical face. Every time Drew sees her he smiles and shakes his head and puts his hand on my shoulder and squeezes it.

Like Hope, Erica modeled as a child. And there's this photograph of her in a floral dress with a white flat-rimmed hat standing in a field, and her face looks very old, very mature. I think it's because she's the oldest of five girls, and I would imagine that being the oldest of five girls makes you old very quickly. Erica is twenty-four and she lives with her divorced mom who is now remarried to a friendly guy with a round belly and hair plugs. The first time I picked Erica up, I didn't know she lived with her mom, and my face turned red when her ten-year-old sister opened the door and her stepfather said hello from the couch, his hands folded over his belly. I thought it was all very strange, and then Erica descended a tall staircase looking like an angel, and the rest of the world disappeared.

Erica grew up in Southern California, Orange County to be exact, and she's really the sort of girl guys get tongue-tied around — she's just that pretty and that kind and that wonderful. She always got A's in school and she thought about being a scientist or maybe a doctor and then she thought about missionary work after visiting China. But for now she sells advertising space for a magazine, and I bet she sells more than anyone.

On our first date, I took Erica to a restaurant called Saffire. I made reservations and held doors and wore my designer jeans and joked with the waiter. I said I was there to help Erica with her questions about journalism, but I was just fooling myself. We never really talked about journalism, at least not in any way that would help Erica — didn't that first night in the coffee shop and we didn't in the restaurant. Over candlelight, Erica asked me dozens of questions, her eyes wide, and I tried to sound cool, saying things like, "Well, when I interviewed President Ford," because I had interviewed President Ford as a newspaper reporter once. But how could I not try and impress this girl, because Erica looked like a movie star, and while she wasn't Hope, who needed Hope when I had someone this bright and beautiful and intelligent?

Of course it was more complicated than that, because really I was still very sad, but the way Erica looked at me that night, I felt important. And I wanted very badly to feel important. "She's crazy about you," Sally said after meeting Erica. "What do you mean? How can you tell?" I asked. And Sally got this motherly look on her face and said, "Cameron. Please."

One night I picked Erica up from the airport, and when she got in the car, we sat there for what seemed like hours. As Erica told me about some problems she was having with her mom, she almost started crying, which is when I said, "I love you." And Erica said, "What?" and I said, "I love you." Erica smiled a strange smile and I grabbed her hand, and she looked so happy.

Erica is very different from Hope. With Hope, I was running around all the time, but with Erica, I don't run around very often. In fact, she usually runs around for me. I'm thinking of the day she brought me dinner when I had to go straight from work to a defensive driving class. I had gotten a ticket for driving in the carpool lane, which is why I was listening to a guy talk about how speed kills. As he talked, his hands moving like a conductor's, I thought back to my hundred-miles-per-hour night on the freeway. The man with the conductor hands said people going a hundred miles per hour in Tennessee go to jail, and I was outraged and confused and had trouble imaging myself in jail. It was then that I saw Erica outside the window, holding a wrapped sandwich. I ducked out of the defensive driving class and took the sandwich from Erica and had no idea what to say.

"I didn't know exactly what you wanted, so I got you ham and turkey. Is that okay?" I said of course that's okay, are you kidding, and I hugged her and kissed her and wanted to keep her forever.

I want to keep her forever right now, but instead I'm standing with Drew in the parking lot of Starbucks—the parking lot where Erica first hugged me that night we had coffee three months ago. I'm asking Drew to pray for me because I have a letter that I'm about to give Erica. Drew reads it, his forehead in knots, and then folds it back up, saying, "You know what you need to do, don't you?" And I say, "Yes."

Drew nods and puts his hand on my shoulder and prays. When he finishes, I swallow hard and drive three miles to Erica's house, or really her mom's house. I park in the cul-de-sac and walk to the front door, and as I ring the doorbell, Erica comes out and says, "Hey," and I say, "Hey," clutching the note in my right hand. "I thought you were coming over later," she says. "I need to talk now," I say.

Erica looks concerned. "What's going on?"

"Can we talk outside?" I ask, and she says, "Just let me pause my video." Erica is getting her master's in religion and she's watching a theology professor lecture about the Ancient Near East on VHS tape. Erica looks so innocent—she's wearing a sweater vest and black pants and a white collared shirt—and again I want to take her and keep her forever and spend the rest of my life making her happy. But I can't do that. I tried to convince myself that her blonde hair and long legs would make me forget Hope. But when it's quiet, I realize that Erica can't make me forget, could never make me forget.

Two weeks ago I told Erica I was quitting my job and going to Europe for a long time. She worried about me leaving, but two days later, said maybe she could come. I said, "No, don't come. I need to go alone," and she got the saddest look on her face when I said that. I'd do anything to never see that look again, but it's not fair to take and take from Erica and never give her what she deserves.

That's why I'm looking at Erica now at the bottom of that steep driveway in the cul-de-sac. I can see the smallest freckle on her nose now, and she's getting that look she got when I kissed her the first time, the corners of her mouth upside down, but I don't kiss her. Instead I hand her the letter and say, "I need to break up with you, Erica. I don't want to, but I need to." I start crying and Erica does too. I hug her and we just stand in the cul-de-sac hugging for ten minutes, crying, and then finally she says she can't hug me anymore, she just needs to go, and I should go too.

*

It's Tuesday when I ask Michael's assistant to schedule a thirty-minute meeting for 1:30 p.m. At 1:32 p.m., I walk into his office, shut the door, and sit down.

"Michael, I'm leaving," I say.

"I'm sorry to hear that. I figured that might happen. You know, when people schedule these real short, thirty-minute meetings, it's usually to tell you something like that," he says flatly. I look at him in disbelief, thinking that was about the strangest thing he could've said.

"Well, I wanted to give you plenty of time to fill the position," I say, "so I'm thinking that at the earliest, my last day will be six weeks from today."

"What will you be doing?"

"I'm going to Europe for a few months, backpacking. And when I get back, well, I'd like to be a writer. Full-time."

Backpacking through Europe was honestly the only thing I could think of doing next, and fortunately I had the money to do it. Others would have called it foolish, would have said that I should've saved that money for a down payment on a house, paid off my car, maybe put it all in a Roth IRA, but I felt the call of some other land, some other place, some other life. Europe trumped practicality. Or maybe Europe was the most practical thing I could do, I don't know.

I thought of all this one night in bed as I watched the rotating blades of the ceiling fan, worried about papers in my cubicle that required my attention the next day. Really I had been thinking of Europe for months—the daydreams of mojitos on the steamship bound for Liverpool, the walks through the travel section at Barnes & Noble—I just hadn't verbalized it until I told my mom one night, "I think I'm going to quit and go to Europe," and she said, "Oh my goodness," and "Really," and "Well, that's different." And now here I am, actually taking the first step, telling Michael that I'm done, that this bad apple is rotten to the core, so rotten that he's willing to abandon order, rationality, a ten-story glass office building, matching donations to the 401K, office politics, and a good salary.

I'm willing to try and make more than a living; I'm willing to make a life. That's why I want to write for a living, because when I write, I feel that I'm doing something I was made to do, not trying to run a program that my operating system doesn't run.

A week later, Michael sends an e-mail to the entire marketing department that says, "Cameron is pursuing his dream of being a full-time author, something most of us only dream of doing." *Great*, I think. *I'm glad everyone knows that. Nothing like having egg on my face when it doesn't happen.*

*

Four weeks after I told Michael I was leaving, I'm unable to sleep. It's a Monday night, and for the first time, I'm actually terrified to get up and drive to the glass office building. Tonight, I'm filled with a sense of foreboding about seeing Michael, filled with dread about what someone might say or do to me there.

Something's wrong, something's about to happen, I just don't know what, and so I stare at bedroom walls. I fall asleep at some point, because I jump when I hear the morning alarm. Maybe I'm full of it though, because the next day, morning comes and goes and lunch comes and goes and everything seems normal. But then I get a phone call and the woman on the other end says, "Can you come to the human resources office at 4 p.m.?" I glance at the clock. It's 3:40 p.m. "What's this concerning?" I ask. "I'm not sure," she says. "I can ask Mr. Edwards to call you back."

At 3:52, I haven't heard from Mr. Edwards, so I get up and make my way to the human resources department, where I hear, "Come in," from behind a cracked door. It's Mr. Edwards, a plump middle-aged man with a closely cropped beard and a gold tooth. "Well, how's it going?"

"Okay," I say, looking around the large office. "This is nice. I've never been in here." "That's a good thing; that means we've never had problems with you," he says, chuckling. "Well, you've already given your notice," Mr. Edwards says, "so why don't I make you a deal? We could say this is your last day and you could go back to your office, say your good-byes, clean off your desk, and make a graceful exit. We'll pay you for the next few weeks, and then in a few days, you follow up with Michael and let him know about any loose ends. At the end of the day, let's just part on good terms, with nothing on your record. You'll get paid for the remaining amount of time you were planning to work, and everyone's happy."

I walk out of the office slightly upset, but relieved that the nightmare is over. And then I arrive back at my desk, which is when I notice that Michael's door is closed, his office black. He left almost an hour earlier than normal. I shake my head. A coworker offers condolences, saying that Michael had told him what happened while I sat in Mr. Edwards' office. I had walked into a trap.

As I gather my things, coworkers give me consoling looks — the sort of looks you give someone who has just suffered a great human loss. Michael's assistant watches my every move, standing two feet behind me, as if I might walk off with a laptop or a computer monitor or start smashing Michael's office with a hatchet, which actually crosses my mind. In five minutes, I have filled a box with personal items and begin walking slowly to the elevator.

But just before the elevator door closes, my friend Kelly runs toward me with a black journal. "Here," she says, out of breath, extending the journal toward me. "I planned to give you this next week, but I'll have to give it to you now. It's for Europe." And I take it just before the elevator doors close, and I exit the building for the last time.

I park my car and sigh. It's 10:32 a.m. and I'm two minutes late. I put my sunglasses on, close the car door behind me, and walk slowly toward Starbucks. Passing brick storefronts, I turn my head to the right and see my reflection in a window. I wonder what Hope will think as she looks at my face, wonder if I look ridiculous wearing my sunglasses, or hip, as I'd like her to think. I'm surprised by the lack of commotion on Memorial Day for such a historic area — banners hang throughout this small Nashville suburb announcing its founding in 1799. Foot traffic is sparse and

American flags stand still on this humid morning as I walk in and see Hope, head down, standing at the counter, balancing a small plate in her left hand. She digs her fork into a piece of cake and takes a bite. She eventually looks up, which is when I remove my sunglasses and step toward her. "Hey," she says casually. "I'm just waiting for my coffee."

I hug her with one arm and say, "I'm going to get something," hoping I sound just as casual. But I don't feel just as casual. I'm shaking as I touch her. Shaking. After I order, Hope points to a stainless steel cappuccino maker, telling me she's going to buy one just like it soon. I smile, thinking of how she once said, "You're not a things person, Cameron," and I'm still not.

We find a two-person table, and I watch her eat. It's curious that I'm even here, because after we broke up I thought I might only see her from across a room, but never like this—just the two of us at a table. We got reacquainted because I forwarded Hope a silly e-mail, and she e-mailed back saying she heard about me quitting my job and would I like to catch up before I left for Europe? I was sad and lonely, so I said sure.

We're now at that two-person table talking about work and books and trips we've taken, when I suddenly feel the need to tell Hope about Erica. I want her to console me, want her to give me advice, which is so weird, getting love advice from the girl you still love. "I was dating this girl, and, you know, she was really wonderful. And then I realized that I had to go to Europe, so I broke up with her because I just wasn't ready to date. The timing just wasn't right," I say.

Hope puts her fork down and looks me in the eye. "Cameron, I'm so sorry, but I'm so glad that happened. I think that's so good for you." "Yeah," I say, looking down at my shoes. I don't really know what she means by that—"I'm so glad that happened"—but maybe she means that now I know exactly how she felt when we broke up. Maybe she means that I've become her. And maybe I have. And then Hope says we really had something and she misses that. I smile and say, "Yeah," but as I say it, I realize something: I still love Hope, but I'm not in love with her. I'm okay. I'm alive.

As I'm thinking this, a woman in her early twenties walks by and says, "Hey." Hope stops talking, and we both look up. I swallow hard and my face turns white. "Who's this?" asks the woman, gesturing toward Hope. "Um, Hope, this is Cara. Cara is Erica's sister . . . Erica, the girl I was just telling you about." Cara says, "So nice to meet you," and shakes Hope's hand and then says to me, almost under her breath, "Erica's outside, just so you know, but I don't think she's coming in."

Two minutes later, Tara walks by our table, saying, "Cameron!" and then asks, "Who's this?" Tara is Erica's nineteen-year-old sister. "Tara, this is Hope," I say. "Reeeallly? Wow. Well, how do you two know each other?" Tara asks, smiling the fakest smile I've ever seen. She's talking so loudly, people around us are looking over their shoulders.

"How do we know each other?" I say, repeating the question, trying to buy myself some time. I look at Hope for counsel, but she's just biting her bottom lip, shaking her head. "We are . . . old friends," I finally say. "Well, that's so great you're getting reacquainted," Tara says with loads of forced enthusiasm.

Finally, Tara leaves, and almost unbelievably, Brooke walks by. Brooke is Erica's seventeen-year-old sister. We endure the same line of questioning, and I'm at a loss for words when the storm is over, finally saying, "I have no idea why that happened . . . or why . . ."

"They're just young, Cameron," Hope says dismissively.

"Yeah."

Hope and I talk for the next hour and a half. I try to forget what happened with Erica's sisters, but I'm a bit shaken up because I know how hurt Erica is and how hurt her sisters are for her, and I want to make it all better, want to run to Erica and say that I'm so sorry, I didn't know what I was doing, can you wait until after Europe? I know I can't do this, but it's what I want to do. After finishing a story, Hope says, "I'm hungry, do you want to get lunch?" And I pause and say, "I think I'm just going to go home."

I surprise myself by saying this. In the past, I would've agreed with anything Hope said or suggested, but not now. Hope cocks her head and says, "Yeah, I guess I should go too." Standing, I give Hope a hug and walk away.

CHAPTER 8

A TIME TO HEAL

As you do not know the path of the wind, or how the body is formed in a mother's womb, so you cannot understand the work of God, the Maker of all things.[1]

Sally and I are on our way to search for the bishop, which makes it sound like the bishop is lost, but what I mean is the Episcopal diocese of Tennessee is looking for a new head honcho because the current one is retiring. Sally, being a longstanding youth minister in the diocese, was asked to serve on the selection committee, and she's the youngest person on the committee by about twenty years.

We're driving to a hotel in downtown Nashville to meet three candidates and their wives, Sally bringing me along as her date and official schmoozer. "Cameron, I'm an introvert, but you're so good in settings like this," she says, grasping my wrist as we drive. "They're going to love you."

I've been attending an Episcopal church called St.

Bartholomew's, or St. B's for short, ever since I arrived in Nashville. I was encouraged to go to St. B's by a Southern Baptist preacher's daughter of all people, encouraged even though I had never been to an Episcopal church. But this Southern Baptist preacher's daughter, knew my background — Baptist church upbringing, Lutheran grade-school kid, Catholic high school graduate — and insisted I go. "It's a very healing place, and a lot of people from evangelical backgrounds go there," she said. "And being someone who also has a liturgical background, you'll probably really appreciate it."

Though I attended mass from time to time in high school, and Lutheran church occasionally in grade school, I grew up in an evangelical church. My evangelical church had aqua-colored carpeting and nondescript stained glass windows and a brown leather couch in the men's restroom where old men would sit. It wasn't a liturgical church, so unlike mass, it was short on ritual but long on personal testimonies and personal Bible reading and personal evangelism, and sometimes people sang solos like "People Need the Lord" while ushers collected wooden offering plates filled with cash.

It was a place with Bible-based preaching, which meant lots of verse-by-verse exposition, so instead of a sermon series on "What God Says About Marriage," as some evangelical churches were known for, it was more like this: "We're going to go through the book of Romans, so turn in your Bibles to Romans chapter 1." The broad-shouldered pastor would then say something like, "I think God's Word is really going to open up for you as we spend the next three hours together," and people would laugh because church wasn't supposed to last three hours, and the pastor would quietly chuckle and take off his watch and place it next to his Bible. We would then listen to that baritone-voiced preacher speak from his tall wooden pulpit, and I would occasionally catch parishioners checking their watches as it approached noon. I couldn't really blame them, because everyone knew church was supposed to end at noon, and it was up to the pastor to keep his end of the bargain.

I use the word "parishioner" now, but I didn't really use that word back then, nor did anyone else I knew. A kid at my Protestant grade school asked why the word "PARISH" was on the first page of our spelling books, right underneath the word "NAME," and our teacher, who was 150 years old, explained that "parish" was a word Catholics used for "church." We thought that was funny. Why didn't they just call it church? But the teacher wouldn't say why.

I went to that Bible-based church every Sunday, had to, and sat next to my parents. But when I was finally old enough to get out from under my dad's arm, which would come down on my shoulder like a fallen tree, I began sitting with Steve. Steve was my age and had brown hair and "skater bangs," a hairstyle skateboarders wore in the late eighties. Skater bangs were cool, but I didn't dare wear my hair that way because I didn't really know how to skate, and if someone found out I didn't know how to skate but had skater bangs, I'd be called a "poser," and that was about the worst thing someone could call you.

Skater bangs involved growing your bangs just long enough to cover one eye, sort of like an eye patch, and Steve pulled it off remarkably well. I'm not sure why he never needed corrective bifocals, because his right eye got virtually no use at all, and I know that sometimes that causes lazy eye. In fact, there was such a thick clump of hair covering his right eye that I imagined scissors getting stuck in there like a lawn mower in knee-deep grass if anyone tried to cut it.

Steve and I were probably thirteen when we started sitting together, and we would always head for the back, which was almost like sitting in the parking lot because we sat in the last row of the church balcony, and from there, you needed binoculars. With those skater bangs, Steve could hardly see anything from the front row, much less from thirty yards away, and that was exactly the point. We were rebellious, didn't care what was going on, and so we sat back there every Sunday for two years.

Behind us was a windowsill covered with dozens of dead black flies, and one time, Steve took an envelope and made a sign that said, "Where a Fly Goes to Die," and propped it up on the windowsill and we laughed. But I thought he might as well have propped up a sign in front of church that said, "Where People Go to Die." But we only wished that were the case, because death would've been a welcome alternative to those headache-inducing sermons and hymn after hymn of what seemed to us funeral music.

There was a sign above the door of the church that you could see as you left, and it said, "You are now entering the mission field," but it felt more like leaving jail than entering the mission field because it was sweet freedom to throw my Bible in the backseat of the car and get home and take off my church clothes and watch football on television.

I think of these things as Sally and I step through the spinning glass doors of the hotel and take the elevator to the fifth floor, where the candidates and their wives are eating cheese and drinking wine with members of the selection committee.

It's strange that I feel so at home in the Episcopal church, or at least at home at St. Bartholomew's, because I've never liked church. I remember driving to St. B's one morning, thankful to have found that community of people, when a verse came to mind: "I rejoiced with those who said to me, 'Let us go to the house of the LORD.'"[2] And wouldn't you know it, we sang a song with those very words later that morning, and I thought it was all very mystical and strange, though most people would've just called it a coincidence.

I don't blame the evangelical church I grew up in for me not liking church. The people at that church are some of the best people on the planet. There's Betty, a sixty-something, rotund woman with thick glasses who I don't know well, but I'll be darned if she still doesn't hug me every time I see her and tell me she's praying for me. And then there's John and Alice, who sit in the same pew every Sunday, and whenever you speak to them, they radiate kindness and goodness and you walk away feeling better about the world without really knowing why.

And then there are my parents. My parents have served in almost every capacity in that church, from Vacation Bible School teacher to theater director to nursery worker to Sunday school teacher to Bible study leader to cook to Roman soldier in the Christmas pageant. They've been members there since I was a baby, maybe before, and my dad still gets up at some ridiculously early hour on Saturdays to attend a two-hour church meeting about heaven-knows-what and then comes home and mows the grass and cleans the kitchen and tries to fix something.

My mom called me the other day to tell me she was on a committee to help the church do a better job connecting with people in their twenties. She wondered if I had any suggestions, and for some reason, I almost started crying. I don't know why, but I guess I just love my mom, and I also know how boring church seemed as a teenager, how I still don't connect with their style of worship, but how wonderful the people are and what an example they've been to me. And the fact that they want to do a better job reaching out to people my age makes me respect them more than I can say.

For a while, I felt guilty that I didn't go to a Baptist church, because I like making people happy, and I wanted my parents to be happy, but one day I realized that my parents didn't really care where I went — heck, they were the ones who sent me to the Lutheran grade school and Catholic high school. To some ultra-conservative evangelicals, they might as well have grown dread-locks and supported the ACLU because that was pretty liberal of them, but they're not very liberal at all, though my dad, while never campaigning for the position, did appear on the ballot as a Democrat once. But if I had to guess, he would've made a pretty conservative Democrat. My parents were just happy I was inter-ested in faith, and because I was, they felt that maybe they had set a good example for me. And they had.

Really my attraction to liturgical churches had to do with the celebration of mystery and wonder more than anything else. In a lot of churches, God gets reduced to such a manageable size, constrained by intricate theologies or simple platitudes, that there's little room for discussion or thought or, worst of all, intrigue. Some would disagree with me vehemently on that point, arguing that the Bible is quite clear about predestination or adult baptism or any other number of things I couldn't really care less about, and that understanding these things only makes God bigger and inspires more awe and reverence.

But I just don't see it.

That's not to say that theology isn't important or doesn't matter. It does. It's just to say that I prefer the scene in *Braveheart* where Mel Gibson marries the girl in the foggy swamp, kneeling as the priest pronounces a blessing in Latin, to the scene in *The Apostle* where Robert Duvall, a charismatic preacher, shouts at people from in front of a billboard-sized sign that says JESUS.

There's something compelling about saying creeds and celebrating feasts and performing rituals because they have been said and celebrated and performed for hundreds of years. In the Episcopal church, which is affiliated with the Anglican church, I feel rooted in something very old, and that rootedness makes me feel a part of God in a way that I've never felt before. My friend Drew doesn't feel this way at all, but he didn't grow up in a Bible-based preaching church; he grew up Catholic and now prefers a Presbyterian church called Midtown that meets in a downtown nightclub.

Maybe I just have the need to rebel, and maybe Drew does too, which is why he no longer attends a liturgical church and I no longer attend an evangelical one. But what do I mean by evangelical? Because even though we have a priest at St. B's, our priest sometimes puts his hands in the air as he sings, and don't evangelicals do that? And our priest emphasizes personal Bible reading, which is a very evangelical thing to do. And St. B's even has a healing ministry, and that's more than evangelical; that's downright charismatic. But there's something that happens at St. B's during mass or at this church supper club I've been attending, and the only way I know to describe it is to tell a story.

One time my priest, Father Jerry, was at a conference when a pastor of a different denomination—a very conservative, evangelical denomination—asked him to dinner. During dinner, this pastor asked Jerry to give his "testimony," and Jerry told the pastor how Jesus had changed his life. But the evangelical pastor seemed surprised when Father Jerry said, "Now, perhaps you might tell me how you came to know Jesus." It seemed that Jerry was being tested to see if he was "in" or "out," or, in other words, if he subscribed to this pastor's theology or not, but how dare Jerry pose the same question back, because clearly this pastor had credentials, and Father Jerry was, after all, an Episcopalian, and we all know about those Episcopalians.

Interestingly, St. B's subscribes to what I would call a very orthodox theology, very much in line with traditional Christian beliefs, and yet I never feel tested at St. B's, never feel judged according to some arbitrary checklist of what I should or shouldn't be . . . I just feel loved, and that love compels me to understand and know Jesus more intimately. The Scriptures record Jesus as saying that you will know his followers by their love, and though I felt love at that Baptist church, I live in it at St. B's.

I don't really know what I mean when I say, "I live in it at St. B's," but as Sally and I walk into the room with the candidates and shake hands, I'm unexpectedly given words for exactly what I mean. I'm talking to a man with thinning blond hair, late forties—a former attorney who one day found himself in seminary and is now a candidate for bishop. He's someone very important in the Diocese of Dallas, but tonight he's very down-to-earth and he likes talking professional basketball, probably because his Dallas Mavericks are having a very good year. But as we begin talking about my church background and my preference for ritual, he says, "I think some people are born sacramental."

I make this "hmmm" sound, as if I know exactly what he's getting at, but for the rest of the night, I wonder what he means by "some people are born sacramental." Later that night I look up the word "sacramental" in the dictionary, which seems an incredibly nerdy thing to do, and the definition says, "Having the nature of a sacrament," which is completely worthless. Why do dictionaries always do this, use the very word you're trying to understand *in* the definition? So I look up "sacrament" and it says, "Something regarded as possessing a sacred character or mysterious significance."

Mysterious significance.

"I think some people are born with the need to experience something that has mysterious significance."

That's what the Dallas priest really said. And I sometimes think that the Protestant Reformation really threw the baby out with the bathwater, because in an effort to fix the corruptions of the church, some splinter groups began simplifying things to such an extent that eventually God became so plain and obvious and explainable that I sometimes see books on five steps to becoming a better Christian, or ten steps to getting your prayers answered, or the three things you really need to understand about God. Or I sometimes hear people say, "All I need to do is read what the Bible says, believe it, do it, and that's good enough for me."

But that's not good enough for me, because the Bible, for all its simplicity, is an exceedingly complex collection of writings, and even if it weren't, it would still only give me a very dim, small picture of God. I once had a friend tell me I should read *Your God Is Too Small*, and though I never read it, I love the title. Solomon wrote, "As you do not know the path of the wind, or how the body is formed in a mother's womb, so you cannot understand the work of God, the Maker of all things,"[3] and that seems to articulate exactly what I've come to believe. Because what do you say to a mother who just lost a child? Or to someone whose wife left him, and who then lost a relationship with the girl he moved to Nashville for, and who then lost another relationship and then a job.

What do you say to someone . . . who lost . . .

Everything he wanted.

Or thought he wanted.

Well, you could quote that verse in the Bible that says, "We know that in all things God works for the good of those who love him, who have been called according to his purpose."⁴ And that would be true and right, but it might not be wise, because it might also be just as accurate, but wiser, to say, "As you do not know the path of the wind, or how the body is formed in a mother's womb, so you cannot understand the work of God, the maker of all things."

Two weeks after Sally and I had wine with those potential bishops, I'm experiencing a bit of déjà vu, because tonight Sally and I are having wine with those potential bishops. It's the same search committee, the same bishops — it's just that you can't pick a bishop after one date, so this is round two. This is so hierarchical, this whole Episcopal church structure with its rectors and bishops and selection committees and hoity-toity wine events, and I'm not sure why that doesn't bother me more than it does, because I'm sort of a power-to-the-people person, but then again, here I am, a Baptist kid with no job, just a writer now, and I'm rubbing shoulders with priests and socialites and wealthy Episcopalians and I'm not even a confirmed Episcopalian, so that's pretty power-to-the-people, I suppose.

It doesn't make sense why I'm in this home, one of the most lavish I've ever seen, dark wood everywhere, museum-caliber artwork on the walls, tall, straight trees in the front yard, fifty people clinking wine glasses and eating catered food and handing car keys to the valets. Not only does it not make sense that I'm here, but it doesn't make sense why I met Hope and fell in love with her, or why I had coffee with Hope right after I broke up with Erica and Erica's sisters walked in and made a scene, or why I read that book Hope's dad wrote on divorce more than a year before I met Hope, or why I took that job and then hated it, or why my wife left.

I'm in a plush leather chair, eating shrimp from a plastic

plate, and I see Sally to my left, talking to some woman with blue hair in an ironed dress. Suddenly a man balancing a drink and a plastic plate deposits himself in the plush leather couch to my right with a thud. He's wearing a suit and tie, has thin gray hair and glasses, and is probably in his early sixties. But there's something in his face—maybe it's his coloring, maybe it's his expression—that gives him a very youthful appearance.

"Hello," I say, dipping shrimp in red cocktail sauce. "Why, hello," he responds cheerily. He tells me his name is Richard and that he's a priest in the diocese. He was ordained an Anglican priest in England but has spent much of his adult life in the United States as an Episcopal priest. "It's strange, because you look familiar," I say. And he says, "Maybe you've seen me on television . . . my wife and I have a solar-powered house." I say, "Yes, that's it, I've seen you on the local news," and he grimaces and looks quizzically into the distance and says, "I think they've done three or four reports on us over the years. There's no end to the interest people have in that solar-powered house."

Richard and I talk for the rest of the night about politics and church and church politics and even about the book I wrote on my divorce, and Richard says he's going to buy a copy. I doubt he will, but the next week, Sally is telling me how much Richard liked me and maybe he could be my spiritual director and that Richard just ordered my book. I think this is all quite fortuitous and wonderful, and who wouldn't want to have a cheerful British priest in his early sixties as a spiritual director? But then I say, "Sally, what in the world is a spiritual director?" And Sally says, "Well, they help you navigate life, but really they just listen for those things God is already doing in your life, things you might not otherwise hear."

*

Three weeks after talking to that British priest, the one Sally said should be my spiritual director, I'm not sure what God is doing in my life as I roll out of bed and reach for my cell phone. There's a piece of paper on the kitchen table with a phone number scribbled on it, and I put those digits into my phone and get a receptionist, who patches me through to a radio DJ. I'm about to do an interview about my first book, and as I'm on hold, I look at the clock, which says 6:58 a.m. I close my eyes and wonder what the point of this interview is. It's a small station, and even if it were a big one, no one seems to listen to these Christian radio stations, at least not the ones that have me on to talk about divorce. Fifteen minutes later, the interview over, I rub my eyes and turn on my computer and pull up my e-mail. Borders Rewards has sent me an e-mail. Delete. DetroitTigers.com has sent me an e-mail. Delete. I get up and do something else, but twenty minutes later, I check e-mail one more time.

And then I see it.

Subject: Today's Interview

Cameron,

I just heard your interview on the radio station, and when I heard it, I had to pull over to the side of the road because I was crying so hard. My husband and I are on the brink of divorce and I didn't think anyone else knew how badly I was hurting or what I was feeling, and then I heard you. I used to be a Christian. I'm not so much anymore, but sometimes I turn on the Christian radio station just because I need something positive. And when I heard you, I knew I was supposed to be listening at that very moment, and all I could do was cry. Thank you so much for what you said.

Deborah

I didn't want to do that stupid interview on that crappy little radio station, but now, for the first time ever, I feel God sitting in the room with me, and suddenly, I understand why I did the interview. Suddenly, I don't care about the pain, the hurt. It was all worth it. It all makes sense — the divorce, the breakups, the lost job. I can't explain it, but on some level, right now, it makes sense. And now I'm crying — a noiseless, body-shaking crying — and I can't stop.

And for some reason, I keep mouthing "thank you" through the tears.

CHAPTER 9

A TIME TO MOURN

Frustration is better than laughter, because a sad face is good for the heart.[1]

It's early June and I'm headed to Europe in four weeks.

I'm done driving to the glass office building, so I spend my days writing, or walking, or sometimes just sitting outside, trying to breathe deeply. It's strange, because for having so much free time, I've seen very little of my friends lately, and the ones I have seen, I feel I'm doing a disservice. The other night I sat with Rory at an outdoor table at Jackson's and it was quiet, the early evening sky red. We watched people drinking and talking around us, but unlike our normal conversations, the ones filled with life, this one was barely breathing.

Usually Rory and I look around the restaurant, zero in on a table, and make wild predictions about the people at that table. "She's wearing a funky hat, but she's wearing it very conservatively. She's more practical than she used to be, but still very artsy," Rory might say. "She also had this gothic phase in high school where she wore black lipstick, sat in the back of class, and hung out with older guys." It's a game that is supposed to end with what Rory calls "The Confrontation," where we actually tell these strangers about their lives. The idea of "The Confrontation" makes me laugh because it's so absurd. But tonight there will be no wild predictions, no confrontations, and no laughter, because my eyes are clear and glassy and I couldn't even see my smile lines in the mirror as I ran my hand through my hair earlier.

"You're different," Rory says, rocking back in his chair. "Not yourself." I admit as much, saying I'm out of sorts, "a bit depressed, actually." I excuse myself before 10 p.m., strange for a cloudless, seventy-five-degree Friday night, because I feel like a parasite, eating away at Rory's energy and enthusiasm. I watch Rory walk back to his car slower than he did walking from it, and I think about how I need to stop bothering people. Tonight I'm the sad clown, and I was yesterday, too, and the day before that, and the day before that.

What am I depressed about? The unknown, the what will I do when I come back from Europe, the why couldn't I make the job work, why couldn't I keep Hope, why can't I stay with Erica. It's all of that, and it probably doesn't help that I've been listening to a lot of Bruce Springsteen lately. I don't know much about The Boss, but I do know this: He's been in dark places—couldn't write the sort of music he writes if he hadn't been. On the surface, he has it all—fame, money, critical acclaim—but having it all feels pretty empty sometimes.

I'm listening to "The Hitter" from Springsteen's *Devils and Dust* album as I leave Jackson's tonight and cut across a parking lot. "The Hitter" is a dark song about a kid who runs from the law, heads to New Orleans, and becomes a boxer. He never deals with the pain of his life and, instead, inflicts it on others. "Well the bell rang and rang and still I kept on/ 'Till I felt my glove leather slip 'tween his skin and bone."

The boxer has this pain that he doesn't want to work through, maybe can't work through, so he decides to give it to someone else. Make someone else feel it. It's interesting because in boxing you *can* make someone else feel it; there's no surrogate for aggression, not like there is in baseball. In baseball, if I want to dominate someone, I hit the ball into the upper deck. I hit the baseball. In boxing, if I want to dominate someone, I hit that person in the face. I hit their face. I hit them until they fall and can't get up. Listening to the song tonight, I want to be that boxer, want to push my feelings to the far corners of my heart's map. I want to beat the crap out of someone, want someone to feel my pain. I want to stop talking and writing about feelings, to never again be called deep or sensitive.

The problem is that this sort of thing is terribly unfulfilling. Springsteen says as much in the song. As the boxer continues his life of diverted anger and pain, stepping back into the ring one more meaningless time, it's clear that it's very empty. The last line is, "I move hard to the left and I strike to the face."

The rhythmic sadness of the song rattles through my soul as I merge onto Interstate 65 and head south toward my suburban apartment complex. I keep playing the song again and again because it speaks of pain that can hardly be articulated by words alone. I suppose the things that Springsteen *doesn't* say perhaps say it all, and maybe only someone who knows darkness—the sort of darkness that sees no hope, no light, no crack in the door—can fully understand what The Boss is talking about.

I felt that way—no light, no crack in the door—last week in church. As the music played—the organ joining in with the guitar, the ancient and the modern fusing together in a moment of quiet reverence and raucous noisiness—I could only say one thing.

"My heart is filled with pain."

I whispered it through tears, head bowed, my forehead touching the pew in front of me. The music continued playing, people streaming past me to take communion, and as my turn came, I walked to the front of the church. As I waited in line, the usher nodded in my direction, and I took my position, kneeling at the railing, head bowed, hands extended, waiting to receive with no energy to give. I took the bread and chewed. I drank from the cup and swallowed hard. I thought about Jesus—his suffering, his pain—but again was overwhelmed with the phrase, "My heart is filled with pain."

I thought of Hope walking along the beach, pushing a strand of hair from her mouth. I thought of picking up Erica from the airport and sitting in the car, her face half-dark, half-illuminated and saying, "I love you." Then I thought of months later telling her I was done. She wanted to know why, but I couldn't say, really. I just was. I felt I was doing the right thing. So too it seemed the right thing to stand that Sunday and, along with the rest of the congregation, repeat the following prayer:

All our problems, we send to the cross of Christ.
All our difficulties, we send to the cross of Christ.
All the devil's works, we send to the cross of Christ.
All our hopes, we set on the risen Christ.

And I want to set those hopes, those problems, those devil's works on something, but I have no idea how to do that.

*

I just got back from my dinner with Rory at Jackson's and it's dark and quiet. It's almost 11 p.m., and out of habit, I flop on the couch and turn on the television, half-watching a documentary for a few minutes. I finally turn it off and sit in silence, and then at some point—some almost unperceivable point, maybe two minutes later, maybe fifteen—my mind lands on this phrase: "I know not Nashville."

I repeat it to myself.

"I know not Nashville."

Michigan is a land of gritty cities, Canadian borders, and long stretches of lakeshore: Nashville a land of Southern plantations, Civil War history, and old money, of chivalry and reverie, of drawls and okra.

Soon after meeting Hope, I visited her in Nashville. One afternoon, we drove through rural places, creeks running alongside hills and horse farms, mansions and hollows. And as we drove, I saw a long line of ancient-looking stones. I marveled at them, noting how they resembled something from Stonehenge or an Irish field. "The slaves built those fences," Hope said matter-of-factly. I was stunned.

I had never fully considered, or been confronted with, the reality of slavery in America, nor had I ever spent a significant amount of time in a place where slavery was so integral. This was a strange place, Nashville, a place of blood and ghosts—yes, Civil War ghosts—of religion and religiosity, of country music and Southern gospel.

I remember those early visits to Nashville as humid, the nights cricket-filled.

In the evenings there were candlelight dinners, the music of Eva Cassidy, and red wine in stemless glasses. Hope and I would sit outside, paper lights and weeping candles casting shadows everywhere. Bamboo enveloped the porch, the gazebo wrapped in vines and Christmas lights, Hope's drawl easing me into the night. On nights like those, everything was a spell of sound, a cocktail of welcome noises.

I heard crickets.

I heard the crackle of candles.

I heard her.

Nashville was as exotic as Buenos Aires or Paris, perhaps because the place was synonymous with Hope, her city irresistible because she was. She embodied everything I wanted: beauty and grace, femininity and strength, humor and intelligence, passion and creativity, a heart for the vulnerable and a pulse for romance. Hope and Nashville were Southern and warm, seductive and mysterious, night swimming and shooting stars, the first day of spring and the last day of school. But nearly one year after those humid nights, the warm memories of Hope only return when Eva Cassidy sings, or when I smell the scent of wild things I have no names for. Midnight has passed, Cinderella's carriage turned into a pumpkin, Hope all too human, me so unprincely.

The romance with Hope ended that night she sat in the laundry basket, crying. All of the words were gone. The magic, just a trick — a novice's attempt at slight of hand. Strangely, my romance with Nashville lived on because the hope of Hope lived on. I still imagined us holding hands, looking at the Nashville sky on a perfect evening. I still imagined Nashville as dream-like, the place where stars were discovered, romance lasted, and healing took place. But morning came, my dreams interrupted by a persistent alarm clock. The early-morning noises came in the form of a Post-It note, folded once, discovered in a suit coat pocket. It was the number of Hope's post office box — a box I used to check on my way home from work. In my mind's eye

Hope was still gorgeous, her complexion flawless, but all I could see were blemishes.

I deleted her phone number from my mobile.

Hope wasn't the woman of my imagination.

Nashville wasn't the place of my imagination.

It was not Buenos Aires.

It was not Paris.

The realization was exhausting, the sun refusing to be restrained by window blinds, my eyes stinging from the morning sunlight. Nashville looked much better at night.

I thought of the line from the David Mead song "Nashville": "Well, it's not quite London or the south of France / Or an Asian island or a second chance." It had become much less than that to me; it was nothing more than a place where I developed allergies, found a few good restaurants, and realized that I had to quit my job.

Tonight, sitting on this couch, the television off, I no longer see the ghosts, the battlefields, the blood, the romance; I see concrete and overdevelopment, lost hopes and lonely shopping malls. I see a photo of Hope and her new boyfriend. They look happy, and I find it curious that her boyfriend looks like someone worth knowing. Not for me, but for someone else.

I see Erica standing on top of a parking garage, overlooking the Nashville skyline, the wind blowing her long blonde hair back, her hugging me tighter than I ever hugged her. I remember how much I loved Nashville those first few times I came here but how all that's left for me here is pain. In fact, tonight I can't even remember why this place was once so magical. Tonight even the ghosts have left.

I know not Nashville.

*

Yesterday I told myself that I had no right to be depressed. How many people get to travel Europe for three months? Not many. The problem is, I can't think my way out of this. A well-intentioned friend e-mailed the other day and encouraged me to shake it off. "Think happy thoughts, snap out of it," he wrote. "Cam, think about all those people with AIDS. Or those people who would give anything for a good meal. Count your blessings, my friend." I felt guilty as I read this. He was right of course; I should count my blessings, but today I realize my friend just doesn't understand.

If I'm merely down, a little perspective might be in order, and if that's the case, then by all means take me to the rescue mission or a children's hospital or to visit someone with AIDS, but the thing is, none of these things will help—nor will a perfect sky or good news from a publishing house or an unexpected check in the mail or a kiss from a beautiful woman.

This thing I'm feeling isn't just me being grumpy or ungrateful or melancholy—this deep, almost bottomless, feeling is more profound than that. I'm calling it depression, but clinically, I don't know if that's the correct term or not, or if what I'm experiencing is somewhere east of depression and just west of feeling down.

It's like these headaches I sometimes get. They're not quite migraines—I'm not seeing light spots or vomiting, the classic migraine symptoms—yet they're incredibly painful and Extra Strength Tylenol is no help at all. So like I said, somewhere east of depression and just west of feeling down. However, this depression isn't a mystery, because I can trace it to my divorce, the job not working out, Hope not working out, and now, my failed relationship with Erica, so maybe it's no wonder that I feel directionless and depleted and confused and, most of all, just hurt.

These feelings remind me of a sermon I recently heard. The guy who preached it probably wouldn't call it a sermon, but it was. It was two months ago, Holy Week, in a church outside Nashville, and the guy talking was Chris Seay, a pastor and author. When Chris speaks, he usually says something that makes me laugh, probably because it's said in such a dry, ironic way, but then just as I'm laughing, Chris hits me with something I never saw coming.

That's what happened that night. Chris was talking about pain, but he started his talk with a funny story about a flight he had recently taken. Sandwiched between two large guys, unable to pull his laptop out, Chris began flipping through *SkyMall* magazine as a last resort, an attempt to keep his sanity. "You know, the magazine that sells you all the things you could never possibly need," Chris said. "They put it in there because they know that we're Americans, and Americans buy things."

On an overhead screen, Chris showed a few of the products featured in *SkyMall*. One was a leg massager that resembled a cast, the next, a bizarre turban-like head wrap for throbbing temples, and the third, perhaps one of the funniest things I'd ever seen: a $500 commemorative *Lord of the Rings* ring. "Now, I love Tolkien, but if you bought this, let me just say that I hope you enjoy being single and celibate, because that's what you're going to be for the rest of your life."

Everyone laughed, especially me. I've never understood the lure of fantasy. Maybe I'm not smart enough to really get it. I always forget the names of all the worlds and dwarves and king-doms and princes, or who has what power or what ability, or which race of people can make themselves disappear and which race lives in this swamp or on that island. And even if you told me a hundred times, I'd still be confused and frustrated and whispering through the entire movie, or putting the book down in frustration and picking up a newspaper instead.

But then Chris said something that changed the mood entirely, and my mind stopped going off on that fantasy rant and went somewhere much different. "You know, the biggest threat to Christianity in America isn't evolution; it isn't secular humanism; it isn't even atheism. It's consumerism. We all think that if we just had more stuff, we'd feel better. Having a bad day? Go to Target. You'll feel better . . . for fifteen minutes."

Chris then talked about the passion of Jesus, Holy Week. He talked about the agony of the cross and the joy of the open tomb. He talked about how purchasing more things can be a surrogate for dealing with our pain, but it is only in feeling the depths of our despair that we are ever able to experience joy again. In other words, miss the sorrow of Good Friday and miss the joy of Easter. Or, "A sad face is good for the heart,"[2] which is what Solomon wrote in Ecclesiastes. Miss the sorrow, miss the joy. And then Chris said something I'll never forget.

"You see, my job as a pastor is to help people fully enter into their pain."

What a brilliant statement on ministry, I thought. *What a brilliant statement on life.*

*

I leave for Europe in just over two weeks, but I'm currently sitting in an enclosed porch somewhere in the mountains of Tennessee. Sally told me this is the poorest county in the whole state, and I believe her, based on the number of cars that I saw in people's front yards today. It's hazy, ninety degrees, and a fan is blowing weakly on my face.

Sally brought me to this Methodist camp for a few days to give me somewhere to think, relax, and heal from the turmoil of the past few weeks. I feel as if I've taken a sledgehammer to my life — breaking Erica's heart, quitting my job, preparing to leave the country, and uncertain about whether I'll remain in Nashville when I return from Europe.

Camp hasn't started for the summer, but the entire staff is here, and Sally is teaching them how to take care of themselves physically, emotionally, and spiritually. I'm interested in hearing her speak because I've been struggling with all three of these areas. I'm in such a strange place emotionally, and being here seems entirely necessary. I didn't think I'd be able to come with her when she asked me five weeks ago, but then the powers that be delivered an unexpected blow to my ego and asked me to leave my job early, so here I am.

With less than a month to go before Europe, I find myself unable to understand why life feels so disjointed, or who I even am anymore. *What am I good at? What will I do when I get back from Europe? Was it a mistake to break up with Erica? Why am I so introverted lately? Why am I hurting?*

What happened to those carefree days at Jackson's, or the nights Drew and I sat on his porch, talking about life and death and relationships? I remember those nights: the laughter, the rosy cheeks, the beer, the conversations about God, the feeling that anything was possible.

My friend Rob once jokingly asked, "If you could put anything in your pocket, what would it be?" He encouraged ridiculous answers like the Eiffel Tower or the Loch Ness Monster, but I think my answer would be an evening with friends at Jackson's or a night with Drew on his porch. I remember feeling loved and accepted on evenings like those, filled with the idea that people thought the best of me despite my divorce, despite my flaws. I was comfortable in my own skin, able to sit and listen without reservation or distraction. I was fully present, not using someone else's words as a springboard for my own. But lately, I find myself half-present, unsure why I'm unable to concentrate, unsure why I'm unable to plumb the depths of my sorrow and move from an inward to an outward focus.

William Elliott, author of *Falling into the Face of God*, a memoir about his forty days and nights in the Judean desert, writes that we are able to be fully present with others only when we've confronted our own demons. Those who haven't dealt with their demons are distracted (Elliott notes that one of the things that made Jesus so remarkable was that he was fully and completely alive, fully and completely present). Those who haven't dealt with their pain look at you with hollow eyes, their gaze extending beyond your shoulder, their answers trite, shallow, and dismissive.[3]

Last night, I spoke with one of the counselors at the camp, a red-haired girl from Michigan. I tried to listen, but my mind wandered. The loss of my job and the loss of another relationship had shaken my confidence, and when I finally spoke, I did so with eyes averted.

*

"The secret to worship is space," Sally tells the camp counselors, and her words give me pause, forcing me to stop what I'm doing and take note. *So maybe that's what Europe is about*, I wonder. *Maybe it's about space. Space to think; space to be; space to rediscover who I've always been. Space, as Elliott writes, "to die," and hopefully die well.*

Several weeks ago, Rory and I spoke on the phone about Europe. "You need to come with me," I told him. "There are songs waiting for you to write in Budapest." We laughed, and then he said, "Ever since you e-mailed me, I've been thinking about it. But I'm just not sure I can handle that much pleasure." I smiled at the time, but his words stayed with me. Pleasure? Is that why I'm going? Am I just a hedonist, acting as if I'm being led by some deep inner prompting, when in reality, I'm only going because it sounds ridiculously fun?

But as I thought about it, I realized that, no, it's not just about pleasure; it's not even about Europe. I could be going anywhere: an out-of-the-way Mexican village, a rural town in Montana, or a flat on the outskirts of Toronto. I just need to go, urged by an inner prompting to heal, explore, move, and mourn.

Physically I look okay, but appearances are deceiving. I tire quickly and find myself going to bed earlier than usual these past few weeks. I've also noticed strange blemishes on my body — places I wouldn't normally get them: my chest, the back of my head, an earlobe, a wrist. Now that I'm no longer working, I nap in the late afternoons. I've also found that my morning run has become a morning walk.

Right now, I'm sitting in a room with seven counselors at this camp in Tennessee. It's my second day here, and though I know the layout of the camp by now, I feel lost. The counselors in this room are all in their late teens or early twenties, but for some reason, they seem like children. There's a movie on TBS right now, but most of the counselors are ignoring it, sitting with their laptops and checking Facebook, a website that allows students to exchange comments and photos. Because I'm a twentieth-century college graduate, Facebook was about four years too late and therefore completely unfamiliar to me. As the counselors talk and type, I stare blankly at the television and then at my watch. It's 11:00 p.m.

I'm exhausted despite my eight hours of sleep the night before, and I think of how only six weeks ago I might've been the life of the party, laughing and joking with the counselors, but instead, they'll hardly remember me. At 11 p.m. I sit in a plastic chair, wishing I could slowly evaporate until there's nothing left of me. No one would remember what I looked like or when I left.

*

Being at this camp reminds me of my experience as a twenty-year-old college junior. I was a counselor at Camp Michindoh, which I first thought was an Indian word that meant "valor" or "courage" or "don't forget your Bibles," but later learned was a combination of the words "Michigan," "Indiana," and "Ohio." I remember having no idea what I was doing, or if I even believed the Christian message that the camp proclaimed. The other counselors had a lot of confidence, I thought to myself. So much confidence that in their youthful naivety, sometimes the Bible was held up as a road map, complete with mileage conversion charts and topographical details. But today, at twenty-eight, seated at a checkered tablecloth table in the camp cafeteria, the Bible seems so much more than that. It seems more like a parable—true, but slightly ambiguous, raising as many questions as it answers. The "bigness" of God cannot be contained even by the Bible, which makes me think of something author Parker Palmer once wrote:

> Our culture wants to turn mysteries into puzzles to be explained or problems to be solved, because maintaining the illusion that we can "straighten things out" makes us feel powerful. Yet mysteries never yield to solutions or fixes — and when we pretend that they do, life not only becomes more banal but also more hopeless because the fixes never work.[4]

This reminds me of the sketches I make. Without fail, people glance over my shoulder and ask, "Who are you drawing?" And my answer is almost always the same: "I don't know. Do I have to know who I'm drawing?" But I also recognize my tendency to do this very thing, to try and make sense of the world. Without fail, the first thing I ask when someone dies is, "How did they die?" as if the answer will help me avoid the same fate.

And so I'm trying to not figure out this empty feeling for now, but to let it be, and to stop pretending that anything or anyone can fix me. Maybe only God can do that.

It's Friday night, 9:48 p.m., and I'm home from that East Tennessee camp, back in my apartment in bed. Tonight I feel the depression coming. I feel myself descending into that place where everything is dark. I thought I could keep severe depression at bay by taking a long shower, giving myself a much-needed shave, and putting on a T-shirt and khakis. And I did feel better — so much so that I visited the corner coffee shop, sitting on the patio with my laptop, watching the sun dissolve into the green hills. In that moment, life seemed worth living. But as soon as the feeling came, it left. The sun disappeared and the air felt chilly on my arms. Darkness covered every part of me. I tried to run, packing up my laptop and heading for the bookstore, but I turned left instead of right and found myself back at my apartment making a turkey sandwich, watching my favorite basketball team lose, and refusing to answer the phone when my brother called.

The game over, the call missed, I turned off the television and thought about crying. Part of me knew that I needed to get together with a friend, that I couldn't allow myself to fall into darkness. *Cam, you've been here before. Don't let it happen. Reach out—sit with someone tonight and talk.* But where was I to turn? Drew was with Ashley. Rory lived forty minutes away. Caroline was with her boyfriend. I had seen Sally earlier in the day and didn't want to bother her again.

And so I thought of getting a drink, watching beautiful women talk and laugh at a trendy Nashville bar, wondering if they could bring light to the darkness that swallowed me. But my pain was deeper than blonde hair, tan legs, and conversation about why we both moved to Nashville. And then I thought of Erica, who seemed full of light.

I hadn't talked to her since we broke up, but my heart ached for her. I wanted to hold her, to kiss her. I wanted to tell her that the world didn't make sense, but she did. I wanted her to show me the way out of this darkness, because she knew darkness herself—I could tell from the moment I met her that she did—and only someone who knew darkness could help me. I thought of her freckles, her smile, and knew that if I called, she would listen, she would care.

But tonight I tell myself that Erica doesn't want to hear from me. I tell myself that if I hadn't broken up with her, she would've broken up with me. I tell myself that I never loved Erica and that, in fact, I hate her: hate her for loving me, hate her for caring so much, hate her for being so wonderful, hate her for being so hurt that I left.

I shut off my phone.

It's 9:48 p.m.

A Friday.

And I lie in bed.

Lie.

In bed.

And I take some small pleasure in my attempt to put a few sentences together.

Writing is all I have now. It is dark. The sun dissolved into green hills. And in an act of defiance that no one will remember, I say let the darkness come.

*

Today is Saturday and as I order coffee at Starbucks, the guy at the register says, "Are you okay, man?" His question startles me, and I mumble something about being tired and needing coffee. My eyes are a dead giveaway when I'm depressed—they look especially blue and glossy.

And so I sit here in a dark corner of Starbucks at a small table, facing a wall of windows fifteen feet away. And outside, it's a beautiful eighty-two-degree day, the perfect backdrop for lying on a blanket of green with someone I love. But I love no one today. Not even myself.

Returning from Starbucks, I call my mom and tell her that I feel myself spiraling downward, and she immediately becomes animated, asking if I want her to fly down, imploring me to talk to a counselor and take some medication.

"Cam, there's nothing wrong with taking medication when you're feeling this down!" "Mom, I'm not against medication," I respond. "I just don't think that it's always the best solution. Sometimes the medication short-circuits the healing. It doesn't address what's really wrong." "Cam, you can do both. You can take the medication and address the problem, and sometimes you can't clearly see the problem until you start taking the medication. I wish I could make you do it, but I can't."

"Well, I'll think about it," I say.

The clock strikes 7 p.m. and all is quiet. It's Sunday, the middle of June, and I'm watching children in the apartment pool just outside my window, their sounds muffled by glass. They seem so happy, the weather so perfect. The children make me think of friends, but no one had called me for several days. I'm unhappy and relieved—unhappy to be unwanted, relieved that I won't burden anyone with my pain like I did with Rory recently.

I can't think of anything interesting to do, so I walk a few blocks down the road for a sandwich. I'm not hungry, but it's dinnertime and I know I should eat. The air is the temperature of bathwater, the light the color of sidewalk chalk. I find a restaurant and buy a sub with ranch dressing. Sitting at an outdoor table, alone, I watch the sun dissolve into green hills, just as I did the night before.

Tonight is just as painful, my entire body aching with sadness. And yet there's something different about the pain. I know that it might be dark for a while, but I'm going to be okay. Walking back to my apartment, I stop halfway, depositing myself on a curb next to the bank. And with the exception of an occasional car, it's quiet.

I guess it's just me and you, God.
I guess we just have to sit here together.
I look straight ahead and face the road, squinting at the remnants of the sun.
I wish I wasn't so sad, but I understand you have to do things like this to get my attention. This whole year has been about me, hasn't it?
I know . . . it has. It has all been about me.

It's strange how I made that declaration to God yesterday, the one about my year being all about me, because this morning as I open my eyes, I see sunlight reflecting off blue bedsheets, and I feel carried, protected, by the most peaceful light I've ever seen. The sadness isn't entirely gone, but I have the distinct feeling that the blue light will do me no harm, that it's the color of water, that it will wash me clean.

It's Tuesday and I'm sitting with a woman named Mary at a burnt orange table in Fido. Fido is the Nashville coffee shop where I go and write, and outside there's a large sign that says "Jones Pet Shop," which I love, because it's not called "Jones Pet Shop." It's called Fido. Fido sells salmon and polenta and popsicles and beer . . . and coffee. Outside, women in sundresses stroll from shop to shop, while guys in flip-flops sit languidly at tables, smoking. It's a humid, ninety-degree afternoon, and the sun feels closer than normal.

With an oversized coffee mug, Mary tells me of her two marriages, three children, and the sadness she hadn't even begun to deal with. She read my first book, which prompted her to e-mail me the day before, telling me that she'd be passing through Nashville. I suggested coffee.

She's been driving for ten hours and her hair is as unkempt as her life—wisps of brown breaking away from a well-intentioned ponytail. It's funny how she probably imagined me as someone who had it all together. After all, I'm an author, and that must mean I know *something*. But I usually feel as if I don't know any more than anyone else does. I just write about how little I know. I don't tell her this, don't mention my depression, but instead sign the book she brought for me to autograph. "Well, I just devalued your book," I say, scribbling something on the first page. We laugh.

As I look into her eyes, I think of all the wounded people I've met in my twenty-eighth year, people who jump at the chance to meet with me because they know that I hurt and therefore understand their pain in some small way. Today, as we talk, Mary's face brightens as I talk about grace, about how she's the sort Jesus would spend time with, and I am too.

"It's not the healthy who need a doctor, but the sick," I say. Somehow she had missed that message. She had missed it between the divorces and the abuse and the twelve-hour shifts and a preacher's comment about how she had exhausted her second chances. And I think of the woman caught in adultery, the one Jesus didn't condemn. "Go and sin no more." No condemnation, just love. Instead, the condemnation always seemed directed toward the Pharisees: the "religious people."

You heap these regulations on people, but you won't lift a finger to help them.

Jesus was a lot of things—just check out any of the billion books written on him.

It seems a lot of people want to figure out who Jesus was and what he was all about, not only because of his importance in the world but also because he was so ambiguous at times. He answered questions with questions. He was the Son of God but called himself the Son of Man. His ambiguity sometimes plays into my tendency to create a god in my image—to create the Jesus that suits me, the one that agrees with my opinions and ideas—and I think that's true for many others as well. But maybe there's one thing we can all agree on: Jesus had compassion on hurting people. The fact that Jesus had compassion on hurting people, the ones sometimes translated in the Scriptures as the "poor in spirit," doesn't surprise me, for I've found that most wounded people are willing to listen, willing to admit that what they've tried hasn't worked.

"Whoever has ears, let them hear,"[5] Jesus said. The wounded hear. The priest at my church says blessing comes with relinquishment, and those who were poor in spirit were usually the ones Jesus blessed. But the religious people of two thousand years ago, like today, were too busy for relinquishment. They were holding too much, making them unwilling to receive what Jesus had for them. They were too proud.

Sorrow, it seems, drives me to Jesus, which is particularly fitting because sorrow was so intrinsic to who Jesus was. Yes, he turned water into wine to keep the party going, yes, he undoubtedly laughed, but he was also the one who spent his life entering into people's pain, which made him well acquainted with it. The

Old Testament says, "By his wounds we are healed"[6] and "He was a man of suffering."[7] Even if these passages aren't prophetic, we have enough examples to think that sadness was an integral part of Jesus.

I think of Jesus crying at the death of his friend Lazarus, his compassion for prostitutes and others on the margins of society, his betrayal at the hands of Judas. I think of him sweating blood in the garden, how he suffered a criminal's death on the cross, and the fact that he was homeless. He truly was a man of sorrows.

Solomon, despite his wealth and wisdom, or perhaps because of it, was also a man of sorrows. A sad face is good for the heart. The heart of the wise is in the house of mourning. The day of death is better than the day of birth. Remember the days of darkness, for there will be many.[8]

It's most likely Solomon wrote these things as an old man, but I like to think of him writing these things at twenty-eight, having already figured out how necessary sadness was to life. I like to imagine Solomon sitting on the roof of his palace, many years before the birth of Jesus, watching the sun dissolve into green hills, his depression stretching with the endless sky.

I guess it's just me and you, God.
I guess we just have to sit here together.

As I walk out of Fido, I look back at Mary, the woman I just met with, and wonder if she knows how sad I am, too. I leave for Europe in two weeks, and Mary leaves for Alabama today. And we could get all the counseling in the world, could surround ourselves with wonderful friends, but in the end, when the sun goes down and the television is off and the phone isn't ringing, we must both say, "Well, God, I guess it's just you and me." I guess that in the end, though I am very lonely, as I suspect Mary is, too, we are never really alone.

CHAPTER 10

A TIME TO BE BORN

All streams flow into the sea, yet the sea is never full. To the place the streams come from, there they return again.[1]

I'm home now.

I think.

I'm not really sure where home is, but tonight it's where my parents live. I'm on the back porch of their brick house, overlooking an acre of green from a wicker chair. Of particular interest to me is an offshoot of the Grand River, the one that winds its way to Grand Rapids and from there empties into Lake Michigan.

I'm thinking all sorts of things tonight watching this river. It's early evening, a duck floating, insects circling, and I'm only now fully realizing that I just paid three months' rent to keep my apartment in Nashville. I really did. The check was for $2,206, which is a lot of money to pay for storage, but I cut that huge check because, though I have no idea what I'll do when I return from Europe, I wanted a place to come home to.

Tonight, I'm thankful to be in Michigan, but it's not quite home anymore, the room I once called mine long since converted into a guest room. None of my things are here, save a few college textbooks and a shoebox with all of those wedding pictures and cards, the ones my wife never took. But my parents are here, and that's something. This is home tonight.

It's peaceful on this back porch — pink sky, summer evening, still air. I hear birds chirping, a chorus of gulping frogs, and at times the hum of a distant lawn mower. The river makes a half circle around the backyard. Lush trees line the river, and I notice how stars sparkle just over the treetops. On nights like these I let my mind go, and when I do, it flits through strange places, over treetops, over stars, and deep into unknown territories. Tonight, I think of a line of Solomon's: "All streams flow into the sea, yet the sea is never full. To the place the streams come from, there they will return again."[2]

I keep returning to the same lessons, especially the one where I get a new job, make some money, get a little attention, find a beautiful woman to spend Saturdays with, and then in the end lose it all. I usually spend the losing times on this porch, looking at this river, thinking, *God . . . I guess you're still here, and actually you always were here, and well, you're what it's all about.* I then try and piece everything together, just like the author of Ecclesiastes did, and I always come to the same conclusion, the conclusion people have been reaching for thousands of years. I conclude that as great as the parties are and the Saturday nights and the laughing and the drinks, I eventually come home where it's quiet, and if I take a second to think before slinking off to bed, I know something's missing.

At times that something is subtle, like not having enough butter for my mashed potatoes, but at other times that something is more significant, like having nothing to drink after a long run. At first it's no big deal, so I shrug it off and go looking for water, but the city is abandoned, none of the faucets work, the toilets are empty, the river polluted, and I sit there on my haunches in the sun, wondering what I'm going to do because I can't remember the last time it rained. My mouth is parched, and if I don't get water soon, I'll get dehydrated, and eventually, well, I'll die.

It's at this point that I'm forced to stop running and doing and making and moving and just sit still and think, because more moving will just make me thirstier, and there's no water out there anyway.

Eventually I start wondering about God because I've exhausted all other options and, well, there is a God, isn't there? Maybe I haven't thought about it in a while, but, yeah, I think there is, and if there is, maybe I can pray and he can send me some water. Perhaps an Aquafina truck will sputter down my dusty street and break down in front of me, and when it does, it will be a miracle, and I'll be a true believer. But even then, something tells me I would explain it all away weeks after it happened. I have a way of doing that.

I wonder how to be a believer, because there was that professor who said God was just a myth. Everyone knows the story of Noah and the flood, but guess what, variations of that story were around long before it was recorded in the Pentateuch, and clearly the Bible is a series of myths, some of them just rewarmed from other cultures, the professor said. And then the professor said the Bible once explained things that science couldn't explain but now can.

It's like that old *Saturday Night Live* skit, the one about the Caveman Lawyer. It was funny because Caveman Lawyer described things in very serious terms, like "that glowing box," which we all knew was a television set, but he had no frame of reference, knew nothing about electricity and cable wires, and so he assumed it was a magic spell that made people fit inside that glowing box. *And maybe God is this way*, I think. *Just this silly idea to help us sleep at night. Perhaps we should be brave and not worry about silly ideas anymore. We're not cavemen. We don't sit around fires and try and explain the world with strange tales, so we should really just reduce everything to laws and molecules and atoms and even to particles smaller than atoms, because mature people talk about particles smaller than atoms.* But that leaves me wondering how these particles got here in the first place, because we always begin where we end, and end where we begin . . . it's all a circle.

It's weird how atomic particles act if you break them down small enough. If you find the right particle and split it down to a certain size and take two parts to separate locations, say Seattle and Paris, and start spinning one in Seattle, the one in Paris starts spinning too, and how do you explain that? You don't really. And how do you explain that I'm thirsty? Not really for water anymore, I have that, but how do you explain that I need *more* than water? I'm sure we could have a million different psychologists give me their theories on why. Some would say that the world is chaotic and my need for God is born out of my need to make sense of life. Others might say my divorce caused some sort of cognitive dissonance—I was told one thing but now believe another, and I'm trying to process that, and people always process better when they believe there's some benevolent force looking out for them. Others would say that I need medication, or just a hobby, or a career that I really love, one I can find meaning in, because that would resolve my need to search for something bigger than myself.

But none of those answers work for me. I need more than water, more than medication, more than the perfect job or the party on Saturday night or the girl with the wheat-colored hair, and I'm not alone. Even the scientist and atheist Carl Sagan looked up. He was desperate for something more, so he looked at the stars.

Tonight, I look down at my hands. I leave for Europe in four days, and the lines on my hands remind me of the roads of my life, jagged, intersecting, seemingly random, but perhaps placed exactly where they are for a reason. Did God really know me before I was born? Does he know me now?

I don't even know myself.

Sure, I know things about myself—that I'm left-handed, that I like to shower before I go to bed, that I like coffee on Saturday mornings, but I don't always know why I do what I do. I don't know why I'm back in this place of lethargy and sadness and failure, the place I've been so many times before. But then I read Ecclesiastes and it says, "To the place the streams come from, there they will return again."

It's all a circle.

I could look at this statement as saying that everything is meaningless, there's nothing new under the sun, and Ecclesiastes certainly says that. But this sentence also reminds me that everything is connected. We begin where we end; we end where we begin. The Scriptures say that God is the first and the last, and so it seems reasonable that nature would reflect its Creator, the waters collecting themselves into lakes and the lakes attaching themselves to the rivers, and the rivers branching into streams and other rivers, and those rivers making their way into oceans. Soon you have an unending thread of water. The same is true in the animal kingdom, where a fly is eaten by a frog, which is eaten by something else, and so on and so on . . . an unbroken chain of nature, one thing connected to another, a repeating cycle.

I look across my parents' manicured backyard, see the lines in the grass from the lawn mower. I look at the river again and, from time to time, see ripples. The ripples remind me of all sorts of things: lines on a hand, the pulsating northern lights, a flock of geese in V formation, the lapping of ocean waves.

They remind me of e-mailing Hope at midnight, desperate for her to like me, desperate like some people are desperate for heroin. They remind me of e-mailing Hope after we broke up, begging her to talk to me, begging like some people beg for money, and her response: "When I break up with someone, I make it a clean break."

They remind me of not knowing how to contact my wife after she left because I didn't have her phone number, didn't have her parents' phone numbers, and so I e-mailed her and she responded, saying she didn't want to talk.

I make it a clean break.

They remind me of handing a note to Erica, looking at the tears in her eyes as we stood in her cul-de-sac, and then walking away forever.

I make it a clean break.

They remind me of a walk I took two months after my wife left, and it was early autumn as I walked, shoulders slumped, sad, alone. Geese flew overhead, so low that I heard their wings flap. They remind me of a walk I took two weeks after I broke up with Erica, shoulders slumped, sad, alone, and I looked up again, and this time I saw blackbirds perched on a telephone wire, and as I looked, they scattered, flying over my head.

Tonight I wonder if I'm connected to something bigger. Perhaps I'm part of this endless cycle of nature, this circle. Maybe there's sense to be made of life after all. Not the sort of sense I could examine under a microscope, but the sort of sense I could make by telling a story around a campfire, a story that's a bit strange at times, but no stranger than dividing an atom into really small particles and seeing how one particle instinctively follows the other when it is spun a world away.

I wonder if I'll remember the spinning of twenty-eight with fondness, my birthday now less than two weeks away. Did I learn anything? Am I any closer to telling a story by the campfire? A story of redemption and grace and healing and forgiveness? A story about how beautiful it is to watch birds fly overhead, especially when you hear wings flapping? A story about how it's all spiritual—the hurting and the laughing, the breaking and the healing—and how this life only makes the slightest bit of sense when we connect everything to its source? Of course, the problem lies in finding the source, because if everything is connected, if everything is a circle, where does the source begin? Where does it end?

"I am the Alpha and the Omega,"[3] John records Jesus saying in that wild, almost drug-induced vision John had on the island of Patmos, all of those years after Solomon. And all those years before Solomon, the Scriptures record God saying to Moses, "I am." "What should I tell them your name is?" Moses wondered. "I AM WHO I AM,"[4] God answered, perhaps the most brilliant yet ambiguous thing he could've said. And so when Solomon writes that all rivers flow back to where they came from, well, how could they not? It's all a circle.

I too am circling back to where I came from, to the source, to God. But did I ever move away from God? Could I ever move away from the "I am," from someone who simply "is"? I think of that tonight, of how I always run and how he's always waiting for me when I'm done running, or maybe better stated, how he's always running with me. My story is so much like the prodigal son's because I always arrive back at my father's house after running this circular track. I arrive at his house after wasting money on loose living and drinks and women, but God is there, arms open.

Solomon was a prodigal too; he ended his long journey of pleasure at his father's house, which is also the place he started. Solomon built God's temple, the most important building on the planet, the holiest place in the world, but even the CEO of God's temple forgot about God. Even he needed to be reminded. Even he ended up broke, thirsty, spiritually bankrupt, searching.

I look on the river and realize that I was born only a few miles upstream from here in a place called Foote Hospital. Thinking of it makes me smile because the part where I was born is now a mental ward. I think I belong in a mental ward sometimes because I get so sad, always have. I remember being seven years old on a summer evening, a Friday, the sun setting. We had just been to ShowBiz Pizza, a place where mechanical bears dance on stage, and I swear I felt this emptiness as we drove home in our burgundy sedan. I felt as if there had to be something better out there, and at seven, what's better than a Friday night at ShowBiz Pizza? But I promise you I was looking for something. I didn't know what, but even at seven I was looking.

I was looking for that same thing two weeks ago as I sat outside the strip mall and watched the sun dissolve into green hills. I was looking for it when I left Nashville for Michigan.

Driving along the interstate I saw an adult bookstore on one side of the road, and on the other side a sign that said "HELL IS REAL" in block letters. I look for it tonight as I wonder what Europe will be like, what I'll see, how I'll be changed. Will I arrive back at this place where I am now, shoulders slumped, sad, alone, tired, depressed? Undoubtedly, I'll return to this place — the only question is when, and how.

I heard a preacher paraphrase Pascal and say that there's a God-shaped hole in all of our hearts, and then I read something Augustine wrote: "Our hearts are restless until they find their rest in thee." I'm restless, always searching for the next thing, the next idea, the next book, the next baseball game, the next concert, the next date, the next weekend, the next meal, the next vacation, the next movie, the next holiday . . . whatever's next. I'm a hamster on a wheel, no further along than when I began. But maybe I am further along. Maybe there's something I have tonight that I didn't have that night in Denver when I took the birthday card from Hope and read, "With love."

"With love." I said it.

And then Hope said, "Cameron, I think it's going to be a great year."

And I believed her.

I really believed her.

I imagine God sitting with me tonight and handing me a card that says, "With love." It looks different than any card I've ever seen. I can hardly recognize the handwriting, but there it is, "With love." I see it, albeit dimly, in that river out there, feel it in the way my mom hugs me, hear it in the flapping of bird wings. Now that I think about it, I heard it years ago from a stranger who prayed over me when my wife and I were separated, and said, "I believe God has a message for you." And I breathlessly asked, "What? What's the message? God never has a message for me." And this man said, "That he loves you, he really loves you." I thought this was lame, didn't believe him, but then I went home, curled up on the floor, and began weeping uncontrollably.

"With love."

I believed it.

I really believed it.

Maybe I really am learning lessons, or relearning old ones, because I believe that I'm loved. Somehow, I'd forgotten that I was, but tonight, I remember. It's not the sort of love that Hope could ever give me or Erica or my ex-wife. No, it's the sort of love I could never shake, the sort I could never be bad enough or annoying enough or whiny enough to destroy.

But these hands of mine, the ones grasping the arms of this wicker chair, *will* be destroyed. This sort of thing bothered Solomon quite a bit, the idea that he would one day die, leaving his projects and ambitions and money to someone else, that the circle would continue without him. *What a great injustice*, he thought, and indeed it is, because it seems as if we were made for more than seventy years on this planet. It seems we were made for eternity, but there was this mix-up in our processing system, because when I click on System Settings, it says Eternity, but I know that's a lie because there's this virus in me that says Self-Destruct, and not even science or health insurance or the best doctors in the world can stop it.

"Jesus wept"[5] is a famous verse in the Bible because it's so short and poignant, and Jesus did weep, wept for his friend Lazarus when he died. Jesus wept even though he knew he'd raise Lazarus from the dead. So how do we explain his weeping other than to say death is unnatural? And who would know this more than the one who created life? We say death is natural because it seems the thing to say, but if that's true, why did Jesus weep? Jesus knew how it was all supposed to be, that we weren't meant to die, but he saw a huge gulf between what was and what should be.

I see that gulf too.

I should've married Hope . . . she should've been the one. We should've had beautiful kids. I should've sold a million copies of my book. I should've loved my job. I should've loved Nashville.

I should've . . .

But all the should'ves are gone now, all swept away in the river I'm looking at, the one that makes a semicircle around this backyard. The money, the dreams, the frustrations: Hope, Erica, my ex-wife, the job, the book, flowing away from me now. I'm watching them leave with the current, floating far away. I'll see them again, but it's dark now and I can barely see the lines in my hands. The sky is black, the ripples in the water like pieces of dark licorice. In the lit house behind me, in the guest room, once my room, is my backpack, stuffed with clothes for Europe.

Because I'm leaving.
Downstream.
With love.
And I believe it.
I really believe it.

NOTES

INTRODUCTION
1. Eugene Peterson, *The Message* (Colorado Springs, CO: NavPress, 2002), introduction to Ecclesiastes.

CHAPTER 1
1. Ecclesiastes 12:13-14, MSG.
2. Parker Palmer, *Let Your Life Speak: Listening for the Voice of Vocation* (San Francisco: Jossey-Bass, 2000), 71.
3. Romans 7:15, MSG.
4. Ecclesiastes 1:14, TNIV.
5. Ecclesiastes 3:8, TNIV.
6. Ecclesiastes 3:2, MSG.
7. Ecclesiastes 12:13-14, MSG.

CHAPTER 2
1. Ecclesiastes 12:1, TNIV.
2. Ecclesiastes 12:1, TNIV.

CHAPTER 3
1. Ecclesiastes 3:1,8, TNIV.

CHAPTER 4
1. Ecclesiastes 3:1,8, TNIV.

CHAPTER 5
1. Ecclesiastes 8:15, TNIV.

CHAPTER 6
1. Ecclesiastes 2:11, TNIV.
2. Ecclesiastes 2:23, MSG.

CHAPTER 7
1. Ecclesiastes 3:1,5, TNIV.

CHAPTER 8
1. Ecclesiastes 11:5, TNIV.
2. Psalm 122:1, TNIV.
3. Ecclesiastes 11:5, TNIV.
4. Romans 8:28, TNIV.

CHAPTER 9
1. Ecclesiastes 7:3, TNIV.
2. Ecclesiastes 7:3, TNIV.
3. William Elliott, *Falling into the Face of God: Forty Days and Nights in the Judean Desert* (Nashville: W Publishing, 2006).
4. Parker Palmer, *Let Your Life Speak: Listening for the Voice of Vocation* (San Francisco: Jossey-Bass, 2000), 60.
5. Matthew 13:9, TNIV.

6. Isaiah 53:5, TNIV.

7. Isaiah 53:3, TNIV.

8. Ecclesiastes 7:3; 7:4; 7:1; 11:8, TNIV.

CHAPTER 10

1. Ecclesiastes 1:7, TNIV.

2. Ecclesiastes 1:7, TNIV.

3. Revelation 1:8, TNIV.

4. Exodus 3:13-14, paraphrase.

5. John 11:35, TNIV.

ABOUT THE AUTHOR

CAMERON CONANT is a former newspaper reporter and the author of *With or Without You*. He lives and writes in Nashville, Tennessee. Visit him online at www.cameronconant .blogspot.com.

CHECK OUT THESE OTHER GREAT TITLES FROM NAVPRESS!

Dangerous Faith

Joel Vestal

ISBN-13: 978-1-60006-197-4 ISBN-10: 1-60006-197-4

A Christian's mandate is clear: Feed the hungry, free the oppressed, and offer light in dark places. Can each believer truly make a difference? The stories and insights of *Dangerous Faith* will challenge indifference and encourage you to actively express compassion.

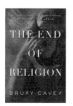

The End of Religion

Bruxy Cavey

ISBN-13: 978-1-60006-067-0 ISBN-10: 1-60006-067-6

Throughout the history of our world, religion has been a contentious concept. But what if God himself has no interest in religion? Author Bruxy Cavey asserts that Christ came to earth to end religion in favor of relationship. Seekers will discover the wondrous promise found in our Savior, and believers will hear anew Christ's call to walk in love and freedom.

Daughters of Eve

Virginia Stem Owens

ISBN-13: 978-0-89109-824-9 ISBN-10: 0-89109-824-0

Virginia Stem Owens invites you to examine some of the fascinating stories of biblical women. Many of the issues they faced (violence, multiple marriages, manipulation, motherhood) are issues of urgent importance to women today. Much has changed since the first woman walked the earth, but at least one thing remains the same: Being a woman is as challenging as it ever was.

For copies, visit your local bookstore, call NavPress at 1-800-366-7788, or log on to www.navpress.com

Environmental Benefits Statement

Active, holistic faith is the backbone of NavPress Deliberate books. We believe that every decision impacts the world of which God has charged us to be good stewards. We are good stewards when we care for people—from choosing to befriend a difficult next-door neighbor to volunteering at a homeless shelter. We are good stewards of the rest of creation by consuming resources wisely and in a way that also renews and blesses the world, its creatures, and its people. We believe in practicing what we publish, so all NavPress Deliberate books are "green." We have chosen to use paper products that do not contribute to deforestation in the world's poorest nations but instead reuse the waste produced by our own consumer culture. The chart below shows the positive impact this decision has on our environment this year.

	UNRECYCLED PAPER	DELIBERATE PAPER	DIFFERENCE
Wood Use	52 tons	26 tons	26 tons
Total Energy	575 million BTU's	450 million BTU's	125 million BTU's
Greenhouse Gases	85,353 lbs CO_2 equiv.	69,542 lbs CO_2 equiv.	15,811 lbs CO_2 equiv.
Wastewater	286,128 gallons	220,501 gallons	65,627 gallons
Solid Waste	34,175 pounds	25,748 pounds	8,427 pounds